Never Will I Die

www.penguin.co.uk

Never Will I Die

Toby Gutteridge

with Michael Calvin

bantam

TRANSWORLD PUBLISHERS
Penguin Random House, One Embassy Gardens,
8 Viaduct Gardens, London SW11 7BW
www.penguin.co.uk

Transworld is part of the Penguin Random House group of companies
whose addresses can be found at global.penguinrandomhouse.com

First published in Great Britain in 2022 by Bantam
an imprint of Transworld Publishers

Copyright © Toby Gutteridge 2022

Toby Gutteridge has asserted his right under the Copyright,
Designs and Patents Act 1988 to be identified as the author of this work.

Every effort has been made to obtain the necessary permissions with
reference to copyright material, both illustrative and quoted. We apologize
for any omissions in this respect and will be pleased to make the
appropriate acknowledgements in any future edition.

A CIP catalogue record for this book
is available from the British Library.

ISBN 9781787635463

Typeset in 12.5/17pt Granjon LT Std by Jouve (UK), Milton Keynes
Printed and bound in Great Britain by Clays Ltd, Elcograf S.p.A.

The authorized representative in the EEA is Penguin Random House Ireland,
Morrison Chambers, 32 Nassau Street, Dublin D02 YH68.

Penguin Random House is committed to a sustainable
future for our business, our readers and our planet. This book
is made from Forest Stewardship Council® certified paper.

This book is dedicated to those who gave their lives in twenty years of conflict in Afghanistan.

CONTENTS

CONTENTS

Rebirth

THERE'S NO PAIN, no theatrical agony. No screaming, no shouting. The kill shot is catastrophic and conclusive. I slump silently on to my knees and topple forward, head first, into the dirt. The lads have seen enough death to assume mine is instantaneous. The lights are out. That's him gone.

The 7.62mm high-calibre bullet entered my neck just below the ear, hit the spinal cord, shattered the spinal column, and fragmented. Since it destroyed the phrenic nerve, which descends through the thorax to the diaphragm, I stopped breathing immediately. My team stepped over my body, into the unknown.

Only later would they try to rationalize their emotion, or lack of it. The continual process of containing the flow of cortisol, the stress-inducing hormone that narrows the arteries while another hormone, epinephrine, increases the heart rate, messes with your head. We each retreat into ourselves, to deal with demons.

When will my time come? What job will I be on when the odds overwhelm me? How will it happen?

We give thanks for sacred certainties. No man is left behind. That's the cardinal rule. I was dragged out of the compound by a mate and a medic. They were the closest to me, and they saved my life. It was business, but deeply personal. The desire to protect one another is fundamental. A casualty evacuation had already been called for. They found a strong pulse, to their astonishment, but had no idea where I had been shot.

They felt around in pitch darkness. The exit wound at the back of my neck was terrible, a mess of shredded nerves, muscles, arteries, veins, ligaments and lymphatic glands. The entry wound, which wrecked the second cervical vertebra from the base of the skull, was a gaping hole into which they had no option but to stick their fingers, to try and stem blood loss.

Everyone in the Special Boat Service is medically trained. We work logically under extreme pressure, by instinct and inclination. The guys' job was to keep me alive by any means possible until the casevac helicopter landed, which it did around twenty minutes later. I've been told I wasn't breathing during that time, suggesting the near certainty of significant brain damage, but they did attempt to force air into my lungs.

It's a void I revisit periodically. It irritates me, because I am chasing ghosts, images without shape or substance. I have no choice but to see things through the eyes of friends and colleagues who were there. They have sketched out events for me in microscopic detail, second by second, but the only tangible evidence of that operation is my Kevlar helmet. It is cracked and chipped from taking a second round from an AK-47, which ricocheted away without finishing me off. Other than that, I have to trust my experience and imagination. The bittersweet irony is that the brain's natural self-defence system ensures that my memories of the night of 13 November 2009 end almost at the moment the insurgents were engaged.

We were more than halfway through my second tour of Afghanistan. I had been wounded in the shoulder two weeks previously, but refused the offer of a ticket home. I didn't come from a strong, supportive family. Those guys were all I had. The bond, forged by the knowledge you are willing to lay down your life for one another, is emotionally overpowering and unbreakable.

What passes as the real world doesn't offer such intimate reference points. We take pride in being the best of the best. Elite UK units select a handful of recruits each year, from across the armed forces. Even being accepted into the selection process is an achievement. Respect is mutual, unspoken, unifying. No one else can truly understand what we do, and why we do it.

Life isn't an exact science. It creates holes that need to be filled. Many in the Special Forces come from broken homes. Some of us have character flaws. I was a borderline alcoholic teenaged delinquent. We represent the two halves of man, made whole. The loving, caring person who wants to do good deeds merges with a violent, near-psychotic aggressor.

An extended tour taxes body and mind, but this was as routine a job as it gets. The rituals and rhythms were familiar. The checks came naturally. My rifle was prepped. Cable ties, medical pack, radio, pistol, spare magazines, knife, and two types of grenade, flash and regular: all present, correct and in full working order.

Orders had been issued with practised formality. We had studied satellite footage of the target, and visualized the intricacies of the compound layout. We knew the type of terrain on which we would be dropped, and in which direction we would land. Call signs were set. Air support was confirmed. Emergency procedures were in place.

Most nights ended in enemy contact.

They began with us piling noisily into vehicles in the last of the light, and driving to where our helicopters were ready to go. We walked up the tailpiece of our assigned helicopter, and sat, left and right, facing one another. Once in the air, we were silhouettes, framed by faint instrument lights. The sweet scent of fuel filled our nostrils.

We had our night vision goggles on and our headphones in, listening to personalized pre-combat playlists. My moodsetters were provided by Linkin Park, Metallica, AC/DC and Seether, a South African nu metal band. The finishing touch was supplied by US alternative metal band Disturbed and their anthem 'Indestructible', the story of 'a master of war':

> Another mission
> The powers have called me away
> Another time
> To carry the colors again
> My motivation
> An oath I've sworn to defend
> To win the honor
> Of coming back home again

No disrespect to pop royalty, but it's hard to get amped up to Ed Sheeran or Elton John.

Whatever their tastes or preoccupations, people really switched on when the pilot began the countdown to landing. Fifteen minutes. Ten. Five. Two. *Whump*. Wheels down. Go Time.

On this particular night we had an arduous walk to the target, having been pitched into stunning desolation. There was no light pollution, so the night sky was vivid and picturesque. There were more shooting stars than I could count. We preferred to think of them as symbols of good fortune, rather than succumb to the suspicion they were the harbinger of a moment of personal destiny.

Eyes gradually adjusted to the darkness. Shapes and contours emerged as hints from what felt like a Martian landscape. All you could hear was the crunch of the boots of the man in front as he negotiated brittle, barren territory. A heightened smell announced our arrival in what we call a green belt, where people congregate around a river.

Humanity is signalled by the aroma of decay. Rotting vegetation, spiced with the shit of several species. Hand-built canals, designed to irrigate meagre crops, feature ditches that can entrap the unwary. The silence is comforting, though when it is broken by the whine of the occasional dog, smelling the scent of strangers, it usually indicates a target is within reach. Compounds tend to be mud-walled mazes.

My mind went blank at the point a group of insurgents moved out of a back door, to another compound, approached by a courtyard, where I'm told another door was locked by a heavy chain. We couldn't use explosive ordnance, because of the presence of women and children nearby. A line of scruffy trees reduced our field of vision. As one of the lead team, I was literally in the line of fire.

In theory, entering a building involves sweeping through a visual arc, to seek out immediate threat. The eyes are drawn into the darkest corners. Experience tells you not to get too close to internal walls, in particular. Instead of ricocheting straight back, high-velocity rounds run along them haphazardly, left and right.

In practice, I advanced into a hail of gunfire and fell like a sack of spuds. No one understands how I survived, despite the advances in battlefield and trauma medicine. I don't know, and I don't think I will ever know. It's a mystery, a phenomenon. The medics worked on me as I lay bloodied and inert on the floor of the rescue helicopter. They put a bag over my nose and mouth, squeezing air into my lungs at a constant rate.

This failed to stabilize me, because of the nerve damage. My pulse rate rose and fell continually during the forty-minute flight to an American base, where I was unloaded on to a trailer, towed by a quad bike. I was incapable of conscious thought, but on some level I distinctly remember one of my mates saying 'We won't see him again' before the helicopter took off, to return to the combat zone.

There is a spiritual element to survival, as well as a physical aspect. I was young and extremely fit, but that couldn't entirely explain why I defied medical logic and remained alive. I am positive I am not imagining this for dramatic effect, but I felt a strange sense of serenity even before I was ferried to the hospital at Camp Bastion, another two hours away, and placed in an induced coma.

I had heard of people on the verge of death being presented with the choice of walking through a mystical doorway to eternity. I blatantly refused to do so. I didn't care if a higher force told me it was my time. I resolved still to say no. I subconsciously ran through a mantra: I will not give in. This is not my time. As spooky as it seems, my memory of mental defiance is stark and graphic.

That's why, several years later, I had a tattoo etched over my chest and heart. It features a lion with the inscription 'Never will I die'. Chris Webster, my childhood friend, has the same tattoo. It has been our mantra since we were ten years old. It is the code we promised ourselves we would live by.

We would repeat it to ourselves just before we did anything daft or dangerous, like an insane jump on a dirt bike, or a gnarly cutback on a huge wave. We fed off the energy of its boldness, and often made each other laugh by repeating it in a funny accent.

Its meaning became more nuanced as we grew older, and life became more complicated. We became more self-aware, more sensitive to our moods. When one of us was down, or having a bad time at home or school, the other would simply say: 'Don't worry, bro. Never will I die. Never give up.'

I've never been a religious person, but the effect of survival on me was profound. It made me question everything, without worshipping anything other than the power of the human spirit. It was almost as if I was celebrating my rebirth. In a split second, I had become a different being. The twenty-four-year-old adrenaline junkie, bursting at the seams with a zest for life and a determination to be recognized as the ultimate warrior, was lost for ever.

A new life had formed, reliant on a ventilator and protected, initially, by a hallucinogenic cocktail of drugs. A new person, similar in so many ways to his predecessor, but different in many others, had a second chance. He's the reason why I want to share my story. It took ten years to place him into perspective. Even now, I pause and wonder what he tells me about myself.

I was quickly repatriated to the UK from Bastion, on a Hercules converted into a field hospital. I had been in Queen Elizabeth Hospital in Birmingham for a couple of weeks when doctors followed my family's wishes, that they should ease me out of my controlled coma. My initial reaction to the hazy, out-of-focus transition to reality was sheer panic.

I was actually in quarantine, as a precaution, because they could not be sure what bugs I had picked up on the battlefield. That's standard protocol, but threatening when you have misty visions of being in a small, square room in which you are constantly being watched by strangers.

I was convinced I had been captured, and was undergoing chemically assisted interrogation. The medical staff seemed sinister, manipulative figures. They worked in sterile, white-walled anonymity, like mortuary assistants. It felt as if I was trapped in a place where no one could hear me scream. I reverted to training mode, and refused to talk to the enemy.

One of the phases of elite training involves survival, evasion and resistance to questioning under duress. My aggression was instinctive fearful and probably exaggerated by my drug regime. I refused to believe anything anyone said to me. I was determined to avoid becoming the victim of a mind job, designed to extract information.

Eventually the medics had to bring in my regimental sergeant major to debrief me, face to face. He tapped into the mutual trust on which an elite soldier operates, and explained that I was not strapped down, as I imagined. I was simply incapable of movement. It was only then, listening to a familiar voice from another time, that I started to believe the story of my rescue was not an elaborate ruse.

Paranoia eased by personal contact and a reduction in the strength of my meds, I took stock of my surroundings. That's when it dawned on me that I was paralysed. I followed a basic instinct and obsessively tried to move. The whole process was so forced, so unnatural. My faith in fate dissolved, and was replaced by another bout of confusion and anger.

What's going on? Why the hell can I not move? This is bullshit. These things happen to other people. They can't be happening to me. It's got to be a bad dream.

My first reflex action was to attempt to move my arms, then my hands and fingers. I was so frantic that my heart rate climbed dangerously, beyond 160 beats a minute. The doctors decided to sedate me again. I was plunged back into a nightmare netherworld of chemical fantasy and subconscious revelation.

Midazolam is a sedative which can induce controlled amnesia. It has proved useful for reducing fear and anxiety in dental patients. Propavol, which is used in the behavioural management of patients with involuntary movements, such as those with cerebral palsy or learning difficulties, is an entirely different dose of juju. It is a milky fluid. I referred to it as White Rabbit, after the Lewis Carroll character that led Alice down the rabbit hole into Wonderland. It took me into a weird world in which all kinds of shit were going on. It was acid-head crazy. I was no stranger to Class A drugs as a kid, but I'd never experienced anything as hallucinogenic.

It took three weeks to wean me off those two principal intravenous drugs. I dropped in and out of reality, chronically muddled and suspicious. Sometimes I would scream incoherently at the staff, demanding to know why I had changed rooms, when I had remained flat on my back in the bed to which I was originally assigned.

There were almost too many tubes in me to count, besides the one leading from my throat to the ventilator that still keeps me breathing eighteen times a minute. There were three in each arm, draining excess spinal fluid from the back of my head, and facilitating regular blood transfusions.

My features were grotesquely swollen. Scar tissue had built up on my arms, inside my elbows and around my wrists, where nurses sought new arteries to drain. I looked like a cross between a crack addict and the Michelin Man. My emotions ran wild, between illogical shame, guilt and gratitude.

My brain was overloaded. At one extreme I was struggling to process my plight, praying that I would one day wake up, soaked in sweat, from a horror movie of a dream. At the other, the pragmatic side of my character took control and endeavoured to put my problems into perspective.

I don't care if I'm paralysed, at least I'm here. I don't know where I am or what's going on but thank fuck I'm alive.

The space between was pretty trippy, and thought-provoking. Somewhere, somehow, buried in an unresponsive body locked into artificial hibernation, a light flickered. I had involuntarily started going over past experiences. Some were distorted, repeated in a blaze of psychedelic colour. Others blurred the boundaries of time and space. I had vague visions and surreal flashbacks.

Weirdest of all, I couldn't get rid of an earworm, a song which must have lodged itself in my brain when someone – I don't know who – brought in a radio to pass the time during bedside vigils. It was number one in the singles chart at the time. Cheryl Cole wasn't my musical type – I can hardly imagine her writhing to an extended thrash metal guitar solo – but it felt as if she was singing directly to me when she promised to 'fight, fight, fight, fight, fight for this love'.

Songs can set a mood, or capture a moment, but this one was

ridiculously removed from anything I would normally listen to. It echoed eerily as it went round and round my head, the only record on an infernal jukebox. I couldn't work out why until I realized that, in my semi-conscious state, I thought she was singing about life, rather than love.

Apologies, since I'm embarrassed by the corniness of this line, but I was willing to fight, fight, fight, fight, fight for this life.

Other out-of-body experiences kept on coming. I clearly remember looking down from the ceiling of the hospital ward at myself and wondering what the hell that thing was, hanging off my neck. Why couldn't I get rid of it? Had I become some sort of android? As I searched for answers, I fell to earth and landed in South Africa.

I was lying on the floor of the petrol station along the road from my main childhood home in Randburg, in the northern suburbs of Johannesburg. Suddenly, without warning, I was standing outside the front gates leading to my house. An unseen force was preventing me from opening them, and going inside.

Everything was pitch black. I wandered aimlessly around my neighbourhood, Fontainebleau. The tree-lined roads were deserted. I lingered on Hans Strijdom Drive, which would be renamed Malibongwe Drive in a new multi-racial nation. It felt as if I was the only survivor from some sort of apocalypse. I was lonely, dazed and confused.

The next thing I knew I was back at primary school, sitting on the back benches with Chris Webster. We've been together since the age of five. His face, along with that of my brother Ben and his best friend Ramon Sherriff, floated by as I drifted in and out of sedation. I was somewhere in there, still alive.

I hadn't been a pretty sight in the early days at QEH. I'd had 5.5

centimetres of my spinal column removed. My head was, to all intents and purposes, being kept on by fifty-one staples, inserted from ear to ear. Surgeons, led by Professor Sir Keith Porter and Jonathan Wasserberg, performed three separate eight-hour operations on me. One was extended by six hours when a specialist had an idea on the way home, turned his car around, and went straight back into theatre.

They cared all right, but were obliged to make a clinical appreciation of the odds stacked against me. They had no conclusive proof how severe the damage was. It was terrifyingly close to my brain. They couldn't predict, with any certainty, the impact of sustained oxygen starvation. The body might have been going through the functions of everyday existence, but I could easily have been brain dead.

The doctors did their duty. They explained the brutal realities of my situation to Chris, Ramon and Ben, who had travelled over from South Africa to be with me. My mother, Ann, had returned home. They had done all they could and now faced the critical decision: was it worth bringing me out of the coma? Their reluctant advice to my friends and family was to switch off my life support, and let nature take its course.

Whew . . .

Every time I think of that moment, it gets to me. It always gets to me. Always.

You see, they were not talking about an inanimate object. Don't ask me how, but I was in on the conversation. The consultants talked about a 50/50 choice. They explained I would pass away peacefully. It would be at least six months before I could speak properly but inside, behind those closed eyes and apparently frozen flesh, I was screaming for dear life.

'Hell, no . . . I need to live . . . Listen to me . . . I don't want to die . . . *Listen* . . .'

Ben came through for me. Thank God he was strong enough to play God. I honestly don't know whether this is a product of an over-active imagination, but I can still see and hear him saying: 'We want to give him a chance, absolutely. Let's wake him up out of this, to give him that chance. Yeah, that's the decision.'

I understand why the experts thought I wasn't going to make it. The stresses and strains on my body were enormous. I had suffered what was officially described as a catastrophic penetrative brain injury. Even today I cannot have an MRI scan because of interference caused by shrapnel left in my neck. It is simply too dangerous to attempt to remove it, since it could shift and cause further damage.

How did I survive? My physical fitness had to be significant. I had always been hyperactive, a surfer, a long-distance swimmer and ultra-marathon runner. I loved that feeling of sharpness, sacrifice and well-being. I was prepared to flog myself through mad gym sessions and endurance events because I thought scouring myself with prolonged exercise said something good about me.

But was there something more? The drive to survive and the desire to achieve stimulated by my Special Forces training high-lighted the age-old dilemma: nature versus nurture. Does the squadron produce the person or does the person already exist before he joins? As so often in life, it is not a black-and-white situation; the answer lies in a particular shade of grey.

I believe the foundation blocks were already there when I backed myself to prove myself worthy of the best fighting force in the world. The training enhanced those qualities, honed them and made them relevant to the role I was expected to fulfil. If you think we are all about bravado or blind aggression, consider the implications of the SBS motto.

By Strength. By Guile.

Strength comes in different forms. Nothing could have prepared me for the mental strength I needed when I was transferred to the neuro intensive therapy unit (ITU) ward at QEH. It was a large basement room, with no natural light. Four beds on each side, all occupied by patients in induced comas. It was deathly silent, except for the subtle hum of the air conditioning and the occasional electronic alarm.

Trust me. If you've been there for any length of time you wouldn't tolerate the obvious smartarse line about it being the land of the living dead. I don't.

Doctors felt I was still too vulnerable to move, even when I gained a degree of consciousness. So there I was, flat on my back, unable to move or talk, eyes flicking left and right, trying to make sense of it all. There were no windows. The lights were on in the ward, 24/7. That was logical, in a warped kind of way, because everyone was sedated to a greater or lesser degree.

I saw four patients die while I was there. Two of them had their life support switched off. Whole families were ushered in, to say their goodbyes. It's like any other intensive care ward; there are only flimsy curtains drawn around a bed at a time of crisis. I had to lie there and listen to the sobs and screams. Parents hold it together pretty well until the machine is turned off. When their loved one stops breathing they break down. It's the sort of sound that haunts your dreams.

One of the victims was a little girl, battered over the head during a racial attack. Imagine the inhumanity involved. Her family's grief tore my heart out. I'm trained to be in extreme circumstances in combat where people die, yet it is easier to come to terms with losses on the battlefield because, deep down, you are expecting them.

Truth be told, I didn't know how to deal with the loss of that child. She could have been no more than eight years old. I had my own trials to endure over the weeks, months and years to come, but the psychological trauma of seeing the guys from the morgue arrive to place her body in a box stays with me, as a reminder of the worst period of my life.

All I could think of was their purple protective gloves. 'Oh no. It's going to be me next . . .'

LIFE ONE

ONE

Family

I WAS AN annoying little shit, rooting around where I should not have been. My stepdad's standard-issue kitbag, a chance discovery at the bottom of a cupboard, was bulbous, made of hard-wearing beige tarpaulin, had a single shoulder strap and felt intriguingly heavy. It carried the promise of hidden gold.

I glanced around quickly, to check my mischief had not been noticed, and loosened the drawstring, which had been woven tightly through metal hoops. The first piece of treasure trove was a pair of South African military leather boots, deep ox-blood, almost burgundy in colour. They still had soil from a foreign land, brittle and desiccated, on the soles.

Medals and badges, drawn from deeper into the duffel bag, were covered in dust. Then, at the bottom, I hit pay dirt: bullets of all types and sizes. Some were in small cardboard boxes, others lay loose. Knowing what I know now, most were traditional 7.62mm high-calibre rounds, copper-coloured with a brass casing.

I was only five, and fascinated by echoes of war. No one in our house gave a damn about age restrictions, so I had already watched too many Arnold Schwarzenegger movies. I loved *Commando*; retired US Special Forces Colonel John Matrix was my hero. He

snapped necks and impaled enemies to avenge members of his former unit, murdered by mercenaries. He rescued hostages too.

Now, thirty years later, I understand the shallowness of such styl-
ized violence and theatrical pain. When blood is shed in battle it
pulses from arteries, rather than seeping from artfully concealed cap-
sules. Old soldiers are pursued to their graves by ghosts of fallen
comrades and the sins and sacrifices of their youth.

My stepdad, Tony Drew, rarely spoke about his experiences as a
conscript on six-month tours of duty in Angola, where South Africa
was drawn into a civil war that began soon after that country's independence in 1975 and continued until 2002. That conflict merged
into so-called border wars in Zambia and what is now Namibia. It
included an equally ruthless bush war in Zimbabwe.

It was the Cold War by proxy, with communist guerrillas attack-
ing supply routes in small groups and dressing as peasants to stalk
South African troops. Both sides turned a blind eye to atrocities. In
many ways it was our Vietnam; the public knew only half the story.
To this day, many veterans feel duty bound to suppress their memories of a brutal, undeclared and unconventional war.

When Tony did refer to army life, usually at weekend braais
where the wives of friends would come armed with cake and custard
slices, he preferred soft-focus reminiscence. He would talk of the
depth of the friendships he'd formed on active service, and the lighter
side of military life – touch rugby on the beach during downtime.
Tales of firefights were off limits.

The situation was complicated by apartheid and the racism of
senior South African officers. The regime tried to manipulate public
opinion by sending largely black regiments to do the dirtiest work;

true equality could only be found in units of the Special Forces such as the mixed-race Buffalo Battalion. Propaganda was designed to stoke anti-Soviet sentiment.

I had no conception of apartheid at the age of five. I was too young to understand that black people, like our maid Sarah, were not allowed into the city to work without a permit. I just thought it was the norm that all the kids in my nursery school and my brother's primary school were white. As strange as it is to imagine today, racial discrimination wasn't even talked about.

I was born in Mill Park Hospital, Johannesburg, in 1985. My brother Ben is three years older; my sisters Natalie and Jessica are younger. We lived initially in Benoni, in the East Rand. An old gold-mining settlement, whose name means 'son of my sorrows', it has been heavily developed in recent years; our small house was on a dirt track.

I attended Over the Rainbow nursery, where teachers were predominantly Afrikaans. They were pretty staunch, and didn't mess around. If you stepped out of line – which, to be honest, I did on a fairly regular basis – you got a clout with a wooden spoon. Looking back, I had a need for strong male guidance.

Family life was complicated. My parents emigrated from England in the late seventies, but split up when I was three. My dad, Andy, wanted to have a bachelor's lifestyle and disappeared overnight. My mum, with three kids under the age of six, quickly settled down, after a fashion, with Tony.

They never married but Tony, a civil engineer like my dad, threw himself into the fray. My fondness for him grew into a deep and abiding love. He was the perfect combination of a father figure, a funder and a friend.

He gave us his time and a regular supply of treats. He would come back from the video store on Friday night with the latest VHS tape, and knew he was on to a winner when he turned up with the new Schwarzenegger movie, *Predator*.

Move over Colonel Matrix, there's a new sheriff in town. How could a kid resist Major Alan 'Dutch' Schaefer, a Vietnam vet summoned from a beach to lead an elite mercenary rescue team against a green-blooded alien?

My stepdad bought me my first BMX bike when I was four, and taught me how to ride it by taking me to the top of the garden. He held the back of the seat as I got on, then pushed me downhill, towards the small driveway, before letting go. It was a classic survival situation. I either dealt with the problem, or fell off.

Damn, I loved that bike. We both bore the scars of my childhood. I lost count of the number of cuts and bruises on my knees, caused by cannoning around in the dirt. I regarded the scratches on the paintwork as badges of honour. When I close my eyes today I can still see my stepdad smiling indulgently at my persistence, and hear his soft voice, offering encouragement.

He wasn't tactile. His affection was expressed in what he said, and how he said it. He was always there when I needed him, and I knew I could ask him anything. In later years, when I was really struggling, he would quietly help me with school work. He helped my brother Ben with his science projects, and built things out of nothing.

He was a grounded guy, who could pretty much fix anything, and was stubborn and self-reliant when he set his mind to do something. He spent hours on his own, mending his cars, which were old and under constant threat of the scrapyard.

He taught me how to fish. He showed me how to tie knots. He bought me my first pocket knife. He literally taught me how to be a boy but also taught me how to become a man. His life lessons have stayed with me. When he was around, it was awesome. When he was away, on his tours of duty, days dragged, months merged. I so hated to see him leave.

He was a short, stocky guy with very dark hair that towards the end of his life was tinged with grey. He had a Tom Selleck Magnum PI moustache, fashionable in the eighties, and, since he was rather flat-footed, walked with a bit of a wobble. Though naturally shy and quiet, he had a wicked, very dry, sense of humour.

We used to laugh at some crazy stuff. Food was his thing. We went through a phase of daring each other to invent outlandish meals; some were inedible but others, like the triple-stack cheese, bacon and egg burger, became family favourites. Any chance we got we had a braai. He loved cooking on an open fire.

Tony used a potjie pot, a heavy, traditional cast-iron cauldron. He would layer meat in it, the tougher the better, and cook it for twelve hours over a fireplace, barbecue or campfire. The trick was to resist the temptation to stir the stew. It was allowed to bubble and simmer, so that the meat almost melted. It created the smell and taste of my childhood. Cooking almost became a performance in itself. My step-dad was a very good guitar player, and would strum along as we waited impatiently for him to start serving.

He was a massive rugby fan, like most South Africans. At weekends we would watch the Golden Lions, whose official name has changed, in our multi-racial democracy, from Transvaal to Gauteng Lions. Those matches form some of my favourite memories. I loved seeing him wrapped up in the drama of a game, and listening to him explaining its hidden rivalries and sacred loyalties.

Sport formed an important element of my life from nursery school, where they took us to a local 25-metre pool twice a week and gave us swimming lessons. On second thoughts, 'lessons' might be pushing it a bit. They lined batches of half a dozen of us along the side of the pool, told us to extend our hands towards the water, and ordered us to go in, head first. Anyone who dithered was given a gentle nudge. The incentive to learn to float tended to do the rest.

That sink-or-swim mentality suited my character. I was buzzing. I loved nothing more than facing a fear, getting hyped up on adrenaline, and meeting the challenge. That was me down to a tee. I was always climbing the highest tree, pushing myself to do something crazy. More formal sport, compulsory cricket, rugby, football and hockey, came later, in primary school.

By that time we had moved to Fontainebleau in the northern sub-urbs, and my dad re-emerged occasionally, usually when he was between relationships. He has remained a fleeting character in my life, but as I've grown older I've appreciated him more. Though I didn't see him that often growing up, I recognize that he had a subtle but powerful influence on me.

It's dangerous to play amateur psychologist, but I wonder whether he, too, was searching for something. Although I have only a vague outline of his life, he was adopted as a boy and brought up in the London area. He met my mum when he moved to Bristol.

He was a rough character, in his element outdoors. He loved game drives, and photographing wildlife. I inherited his free-spirited nature, and we share other characteristics. He was hugely into physical fitness, and forced his love of swimming and triathlons on to us. Failure wasn't regarded as an acceptable option.

We only saw him once a month, at most, when he would take us to events. Ben and I did our first triathlon together when I was eight; he did the swim, and understandably took his time, so I was the last competitor on the road for the 3-kilometre cycle section. I was alone, fearful that I was lost and merely guessing I was on the right route, but managed to finish.

Sure, I was shattered. I felt sick and scared. But the fact that I didn't quit stayed with me.

The lesson was quickly reinforced when my dad entered me for the Midmar mile, the world's largest open-water swimming event, held annually in February at the Midmar Dam north of Pietermaritzburg. It involves thousands of competitors sprinting across a muddy shore through the shallows until the water is deep enough to swim.

The people come in three-minute waves. It's mayhem; they swim over and across you in a stampede to get to the other side of the dam. Again, I was on my own, terrified. There were times when I thought I wasn't going to make it. Yet, somehow, and in some strange way, I refused to give up. I just kept going. I conquered myself.

Dad made us do it every year, and I've never thought to ask him why. I suppose, deep down, I know the answer. I've only seen him once since my injury, in early 2020. He has married a lovely lady named Mary-Ann, who comes from traditional Afrikaans stock. It must have involved a degree of culture shock, since he remains very English in his outlook.

I wasn't aware of outright hostility as a child, but anyone from an

English family is given a crash course in Afrikaans slang. We were known as rooi nekers, because of the propensity of pale English skin to burn in the sun, or soutpiel, which is a more direct, and less delicate, reference to the difference between the cultures. Put simply, *sout* means salt and *piel* means penis. We were derided as having one foot in South Africa, and one foot in Britain, with our cocks dangling in the Atlantic Ocean.

It is hard sometimes to grasp their logic and mentality, but once you begin to understand the conventions of their disciplined society, and the pride they take in their heritage, Afrikaaners are not the ogres many make them out to be. They're a contradiction: they can be wonderfully bonkers and terribly strict. It doesn't take much for their bluntness to come across as arrogance, but they form firm friendships.

My best mate, Chris Webster, gatecrashed my life on our first day at the Robin Hills primary school. He was a long, skinny kid assigned the seat next to me at the back of the class, which, in hindsight, was a schoolboy error by the teacher, who compounded the mistake by leaving the classroom to answer a summons from elsewhere.

Chris and I just clicked. Within seconds we were rubbing our feet on the carpet, stealing up to the girls, and giving them shocks, through fingers charged with static electricity. While they were distracted and squealing, we stole their colouring books and started using the desks as climbing frames. All in all, it was quite the scene with which to confront the returning teacher.

Before I knew it I had been grabbed by my collar, lifted off my feet, and given a thwack across the back of my thighs with a wand, or rattan cane. I'd never felt anything like it. Once Chris had suffered similarly, we were marched off to the headmaster, who phoned our parents in tones reserved for a hanging judge.

The pain faded, parental disgust barely registered, and we continued, down the years, to make regular appearances in the principal's office. Another party trick was to steal one of my mum's packs of cigarettes, which we buried beside the tennis courts until second break, when we unearthed them and sneaked into the pavilion. I'm sure you can guess the script. Just as we lit up, marvelling at how we were ten-year-old kings of cool, we were caught red-handed. The nicotine hit was swiftly replaced by a more stinging blow, supplied by the all-too-familiar wand.

We remain inseparable, spiritually, though Chris recently sold up and emigrated to New Zealand with his wife and son.

Some of our schoolyard games were borderline psychotic. One, poetically entitled Hunt the Cunt, was staged in the so-called 'after care' period between the end of formal lessons at 2 p.m. and home time at 5 p.m. Basically, it involved younger boys hiding as best they could, and being hunted down by older pupils, including my brother Ben.

It was a feral form of hide and seek. When they found us, they beat the shit out of us. We just took our punishment, and hoped to God that the beating wasn't too bad.

We learned to obey orders. One of the older kids somehow got wind of the fact that some of the local fathers were surreptitiously dumping their porno mags in the recycling bin at the front of the school. Together with a couple of the smaller boys, I was volunteered to rummage around in search of a quick thrill.

This was a perilous business. If we were caught sneaking outside the gates we would be in mega shit. If we became trapped inside the bin we would be beyond immediate rescue. The ends justified the means, though, when on an early foray we emerged with a copy of *Mayfair*, which was duly smuggled down to the tennis pavilion. There, we formed a disorderly circle, and gawped. The models might have had stars positioned primly over their nipples, but our imaginations were fired. It beat biology lessons every day of the week.

The chaos continued outside school. Chris, myself and another friend, Bobby Bullen, went through a phase of going round to one another's houses at the weekend. It began innocently enough, building forts from spare wood and household rubbish, but once we introduced barbed wire and camouflage into our tree houses things quickly got out of hand.

Bobby's air rifle was a game changer. We'd climb trees, take up residence, and scramble for cover after shooting at pedestrians walking below us. We were hardly inconspicuous. We fell from the branches occasionally, due to a mixture of excitement, fear and clumsiness, and would regularly be caught. That meant being dragged home to face all sorts of strife.

We weren't bad kids, but we had our moments. It took its toll on my mum, whose relationship with Tony had started to break down. They had my youngest sister Jessica in 1995, but to be honest, I don't know if they were ever in love. Their connection was convenient, and although my stepdad continued to take us to the cinema, and ferry us around, he wasn't the disciplinarian we probably needed.

Things began to go badly wrong. For some unfathomable reason my mother, whose drinking problem was worsening, got it into her head that she wanted to forge a new life in the United States. She sold our house for a fraction of what it was worth, got rid of everything we owned, and suddenly uprooted all four of us. We flew to New York with all we could carry while Tony stayed in Johannesburg.

We stayed with cousins and did cool things, like going to the top of the Twin Towers, yet, all too soon, reality bit. We were herded on to another plane and deposited in a basically furnished town house in San Diego. Mum worked from home for a former boss, who lived just across the border in Mexico after leaving South Africa with suspicious speed.

Something didn't feel right, but we had more immediate problems to contend with after being enrolled in a random local high school in mid-term. None of us had wanted to leave our friends; suddenly all we had was one another. We were isolated, picked on because of our accents, and couldn't penetrate the cliques.

Ben describes the experience as like walking on to a film set where the skater jocks compete with quarterback teen idols, and the goth nerds skulk in the corner. I had my own Forrest Gump moment on my first day on the yellow school bus, looking for somewhere to sit. Most of the kids were in pairs; the few on their own glared at me, as if daring me to invade their space. In the film, Forrest finds acceptance from a girl named Jenny. I had no such luck, and simply plonked myself down where I wasn't wanted. The cycle of resentment, rejection and murmured insults became a daily ritual. It never got any easier, but I knew I had to stay strong. Any indication of weakness and they would have been on me like a pack of jackals.

San Diego is an extension of the American dream, with a few frayed edges. Since you are what you wear in such a materialistic, money-conscious culture, we were vulnerable. Mum was obviously struggling to make ends meet, and we wore the same clothes most days. I tried to make a joke of it when they cornered me in the cafeteria and laughed at my stained, shiny trousers, but deep down it hurt.

The kids' cruelty felt worse because it was delivered so casually. I looked them in the eye and walked off in feigned contempt, but it cut me to the core. Anger and frustration simmered and soured inside me, and I eventually directed my resentment at Mum, who seemed to be coming apart at the seams.

I was twelve, and felt I had to behave as the man of the house. I saw the impact the situation was having on my sister Natalie, who was becoming timid and withdrawn. My brother Ben, a natural introvert, was bullied relentlessly. I saw through his brave face, and recognized the strength it took for him to get up in the morning and face it all again.

It was a horrible experience, and I got into a few scraps, trying to stick up for them. I licked my wounds, and tried to hide the hurt. I didn't tell Mum what was going on since she had more than enough to deal with. Promises had evidently not been fulfilled. The money had dried up. She was preoccupied and panic-stricken.

I've never got to the bottom of what she and her former boss were up to, but it didn't smell right. From what little I've been able to glean, the authorities were closing in on them. We had been in the States for eight months when, in the dead of night, Mum roused us from our beds and told us to pack a small bag each.

We were tired and confused. What was she on about? Why were we going to England, another alien country? How could we leave without saying farewell to the few friends we had found? Ben managed to scrawl a note, which he stuck on a neighbour's front door, but we upped and left in a hurry, without most of our belongings.

Mum drove us to the airport, and dumped the car at the terminal. She must have been planning our midnight flit for some time since our flights had been pre-booked. We cleared customs and, effectively, skipped the country. Twelve hours later we emerged, blinking, into a cold morning at Heathrow, to be greeted by strangers who introduced themselves as Auntie Joyce and Uncle Bruce.

Life was about to become a lot darker, and eventually, much more dangerous.

TWO

Edge of Darkness

THIS IS WHAT scraping along the bottom feels like: cold, bewildering, painful, scary. There's no money, no hope, no home, no comfort. You are unable to afford the pretence of dignity, or the price of normality. You are human driftwood, with no idea where you are, or where you will end up. It's quite something to get your head around when you are twelve years old.

We were driven from Heathrow to Poole in Dorset, where our family was sliced and diced. The boys, Ben and I, were assigned to Joyce, who turned out to be our grandmother's sister. The girls, Natalie and Jessica, went with Mum to stay with Great Aunt Mel, our grandmother's other sister. The alternative, being taken into care, was too terrible to contemplate, but we still felt abandoned.

Time gives me perspective, without reducing the power of the memory. Like everyone else, I experienced enforced isolation during the Covid-19 epidemic, but this was infinitely harder to take because it seemed we had been singled out. To all intents and purposes my brother and I were locked down in a small attic room.

We had nowhere to go, nothing to do, no friends to mix with.

We didn't know our relatives, though it must have been equally difficult for them to have a couple of kids dumped in their laps. Joyce was a lovely lady: she wasn't the problem. Our great-uncle Bruce, however, was a right piece of work. He didn't bother to hide his resentment. He was sharp, sour and in a perpetual sulk, complaining that we were always in his way.

Was he just a grumpy old git, or was there something else going on beneath the surface?

He had seen a lot of death as a fighter pilot in the Second World War, and though it was a generation later, he was showing classic symptoms of PTSD: anxiety, irritability and possibly guilt. He had children of his own – I don't know how many, can't remember their names and haven't a clue where they are now – but showed no inclination to tolerate family life, let alone enjoy it.

We had to deal with problems beyond our years. It was as if we had no one in the world but ourselves. Thank God I had Ben. We were different characters – he loved the discipline of being a Boy Scout while I yearned to run free without dibbing, dobbing or making promises to Akela – and would temporarily grow apart as teenagers, but he was my rock.

We had no contact with our sisters, and Mum visited sporadically. Every time she left, to resume the slog of finding a job and making sense of the social care system, it felt as if we had been orphaned. The only time we left Joyce's house was to accompany Mum to the Citizens Advice Bureau, as evidence of the family's needs. Watching her plead for our future was humiliating, and it still took a couple of months for bureaucracy to relent. Eventually, after another family outing to the Job Centre, she found a part-time job, and received child benefit and enough housing credits to be given a council flat on the toughest housing estate in Bournemouth.

It was barren, but at least we were together again. Mum and our great-aunties begged and borrowed basic bits of furniture, some old cutlery and a few plates, pots and pans. We slept on blow-up mattresses on the floor. The area was as rough as a badger's arse, and the school into which we were parachuted, Summerbee Comprehensive, was rated one of the worst in the country. It was eventually closed in August 2004, and revived as the Bishop of Winchester Academy, which has established a reputation for academic excellence, but at the time it felt like a war zone. I absolutely hated turning up on the first day, and having to go again through all the grief we had experienced so recently in California.

That familiar feeling of being an outsider wasn't any easier to deal with. Everyone staring at you, in the playground or classroom, so you feel like a piece of crap. Being called to the front by the teacher to introduce yourself. Having pupils laugh at your accent, and hearing them take the piss out of your second-hand clothes.

The estate kids were ruthless, kicking, taunting, spitting and trying every trick in the book to get me into trouble. I couldn't help myself. I bit back. I wouldn't let them pick on me without punishment, so I got into loads of fights. Mum, bless her, was continually called into school, where she argued against the assumption I was the disruptive influence.

Gradually, the kids realized I was not the type to take any shit. They knew I'd give as good as I got, verbally or physically. They found it easier to leave me to my own devices, and that's when real trouble loomed. Without knowing it, I had earned the respect of the sort of people I should have avoided at all costs.

These boys were not your good little Johnnies. They were in their early teens and into proper bad stuff: drugs, burglaries, intimidation. They gave me what I craved, a sense of belonging. They offered me the chance to strike back at a world that had no time for me. They saw me as one of their own, damaged and dangerous.

I don't want to go over the top here, or make empty excuses, but a recent survey of orphaned kids resonated with me. It found that 35 per cent of them had severe personal conduct issues. They were emotionally hyperactive, they struggled to build balanced relationships with their peers, and were responsible for consistent anti-social behaviour.

Bear in mind, I'm only twelve. I'm smoking weed at break time, seeing my new-found friends dealing other drugs. I'm learning their trade, helping to steal mopeds, joining in shoplifting expeditions and acting as lookout during household burglaries. I'm seduced by the power of the gang. I'm so close to being lost for ever.

Deep down, I knew I was acting up, playing the role of outlaw. I was upset and irritated at the hand life had dealt me. I missed my home and my mates in South Africa, and resented the fact I had been wrenched away from them on a whim. Petty criminality was my way – the wrong way – of venting anger and frustration.

What saved me was an ability to differentiate between degrees of right and wrong. I was never formally arrested, but I knew that being dragged home by the police and being given dire warnings about the direction in which my life was heading wasn't big or clever. I don't want or expect praise for this, but I drew the line at hurting others. I hung back when the gang mugged someone on the street, stealing anything from their mobiles to their dinner money before battering them. I'd never do that to another human being. I had standards and boundaries, however warped and undetectable they might have appeared. A lot of the kids didn't have those barriers. Quite a few didn't care about anything, or anyone. They took a vicious pride in hurting someone. They were thrilled by the fear in their victim's eyes, and the submission in their body language. They loved the power it gave them. That sort of self-justification is reserved for life's losers.

I was an idiot, but I was different. I didn't want to inflict pain and suffering. I was just looking for a buzz, something to distract me. Thankfully, Mum saw through my pathetic bravado and realized that I was a little boy, acting the hard man. She had the moral courage to admit her own mistakes and act on the realization her children were struggling, badly.

After ten months trying to make ends meet in the UK, she uprooted us again to return to South Africa. It wasn't an easy option, because she knew what folk would say behind her back and, occasionally, to her face. She had been a dreamer, a waster, a failure. She had a lot of making up to do to a lot of people. So it took guts to return to our old suburb in Johannesburg, Fontainebleau, and try to retrieve the shreds of the life we had before she whisked us off to the US. Tony Drew, our stepdad, linked back up with us. Mum had her tail between her legs. It was obviously awkward at first, but Jessica, after all, was his flesh and blood. He loved us all, and we tried to reciprocate.

We rented a house next to Ramon Sherriff, my brother Ben's best mate. It's funny how things work out: we have developed a lifelong friendship, but back then I knew him only as a persecutor. He had been an enthusiastic participant in those feral games at Robin Hills primary school, and used to beat me up after chasing me around the playground. We soon began to bond during a little extra-curricular mischief, and it was clear I was no longer the compliant victim he once knew.

Confronted with the usual nonsense when I joined yet another new school, Northcliff High, a leading co-educational institution in the neighbouring suburb of Blackheath, I knew how the scenario would play out. First day: you don't know where to stand. No one tells you where to go. You eventually find the right classroom. The teacher brings you up to the front. Morning everyone, this is Toby. He's started today. Please make him welcome, blah, blah, blah. Everyone sniggers. A few flick you the finger or a V sign behind the teacher's back. You stand there feeling like a right lemon, and you know what's coming next. Someone will make the mistake of thinking you'll just suck it up when he starts laughing at you. You're nervous, but you dare not show it. You wait for that first person to misjudge you then, straight off the bat, you go *boom*, and knock seven bells out of him. That sends out the message. Don't fuck with me, right?

In this case it took a week for it all to play out. I was sitting in the quad, minding my own business, when this lad came up to me and called me a mummy's boy. I asked him what his problem was. When he started smirking and impersonating me I simply stood up and dropped him with a right hook. He never saw it coming. I followed it up with a volley of three or four punches and he was on his back, cowering in a foetal position. You could see everyone's jaws drop. It set the tone for the term. I could read them as if they had speech bubbles over their heads. 'Shit. This Toby kid knows how to handle himself. He comes from a bad place, a difficult background. We'd better leave him well alone.'

I had learned how to survive on my own. I was at ease in my own skin, which had grown a few extra protective layers. I had figured out who I was: a loner, a natural outsider. I was comfortable with the creases in my character. I was driven to push boundaries, and create a little bit of havoc. It was in my blood. I thought I was untouchable.

The aftermath of that incident was as predictable as my ritual retaliation against that soppy kid. I was hauled into the principal's office. He didn't want a roughneck like me sullying his school's image of bright boys and girls in light blue blazers being prepared as model citizens. I represented an alternative future. He suspended me for a week, which was understandable, but utterly pointless.

The end – ensuring there would be no more bullying – justified the means. I'd started picking up bad habits in the UK, and was ready to move to the dark side. I pretty much sacked off school. I wasn't interested in their conventions or their cautions. If I wanted to play truant, there was no way they were going to stop me.

The only source of regret was the immediate strain it put on my relationship with Ben. He had only a year before the exams that would shape his life, and was told by teachers that he would be dropped back a year unless he quickly improved his grades. That wasn't an option for him, since he had set his heart on a place at Cape Town University.

He applied himself, and tried to tell me that he wasn't the only academic one in the family. I was too young, wilful and wild to understand why he argued against my determination to dismiss school as an irrelevance. He saw something in me that took my paralysis, and subsequent depression, to coax out into the open. I did have a brain, if I bothered to use it.

By the time I was fourteen I was out of control. My adolescent hormones were unleashed. All I cared about was girls, drugs and drinking. It was something of a miracle if I turned up to school on time, or if I made it at all. I'd usually come in at second break, around 12.30 p.m., hung over from the night before. I'd mooch about for a couple of hours to ensure I was noticed, before heading who knows where.

I was smart enough to try to play the system. When I failed to answer my name when the register was called in the morning, I would be marked down as being late or absent on a paper chit that was ferried to the library to be computerized. Attendance statistics would be compiled over the course of the term, and in my case would be damning. My cunning plan involved befriending the disabled lad charged with inputting the data. He suffered badly from childhood polio, and was shunned by most of the other pupils. He was a gentle soul and I genuinely liked him, but I also exploited his innocence. When I asked, he willingly changed the records to show that I was present, most days.

It took a while for the teachers to spot the ruse. They began making their own notes, cross-checking their experiences of my unreliability, and the game was up. They announced, with a severity that I took to be pomposity, that they knew what I had been up to. They didn't know the half of it.

South Africa consumes the most beer of any African nation, an average of 90 litres per person, annually. I was getting through that in a couple of months, and defying advice not to go into the townships to do so. My favourite drink was coarse beer, sold in 750ml containers in illegal shebeens that were officially off limits to white kids.

I loved Umqombothi, a beer traditionally prepared over a fire by the Xhosa and Zulu. Made from corn, maize malt, sorghum malt, yeast and water, it is thick, creamy and a little chewy. It smells faintly sour, and is light tan in colour. Apparently it is also rich in vitamin B but, trust me, that is not its main selling point.

We were warned off the shebeens, shacks that sold raw alcohol and a range of drugs including weed, skunk, cocaine, ecstasy and LSD. They can be scary places, but I didn't give a shit. Perhaps it was the confidence of youth, which generates a foolish sense of invulnerability. Perhaps it was just the arrogance of an ignorant, mixed-up kid.

When I walked in, and sat down with the locals, I felt a sense of acceptance and allegiance. You'd think they'd treat a gobby teenager with suspicion, even contempt. Yet there was no malice. They welcomed me on my own terms: 'Cool, man. Come sit down, crack a coarse. There you go. Sweet. You crack on and do your thing.'

I was too self-obsessed to appreciate the undercurrents of unease, which bubbled to the surface when a black school mate of Chris Webster's invited us to his home in Soweto. His family lived ten to two rooms, but shared what they cooked in a communal pot before taking us into the local shebeen. Chris and I were feeling pretty out there, shooting the shit with about twenty guys, when his mate came up to us with a scared look in his eyes.

'We need to go now.'

'Why? What's the problem?'

'Trust me. We need to leave.'

With that, we were bundled out of the tin door at the back of the shack and into our friend's home. A local gang had heard of our presence, and were threatening to shoot us. When they burst in they were confronted by half a dozen adults, all strangers who sought to protect us. As a brawl broke out, we made a run for it.

Despite our problems in the US and UK, I'd had a relatively comfortable upbringing. Nothing had prepared me for the poverty I saw in townships like Soweto, Alexandria and Diepsloot, which were close to but existed outside the bubble of affluent white suburbs like Fontainebleau, Sandton and Dainfern. We were told to stay away from such settlements. Was the stigma of visiting them a by-product of guilt or prejudice within a privileged white community in a post-apartheid world? Probably a bit of both.

So much has changed for the better in modern multi-racial South Africa, but what sort of society accepts the privations of a settlement like Diepsloot, where the majority of the two hundred thousand residents in what was once a transit camp are without running water, sanitation and electricity? Why should families be expected to live in shacks measuring 3 metres by 2, made of scrap metal, wood, plastic and cardboard, which flood in the summer rains?

Crime is rampant, and vigilantes operate with deadly impunity. This might not make much sense, but I hated seeing such poverty, and loved being there to see it. I was without a moral compass in so many areas of my life as a teenager, but I knew it was wrong. It ripped my heart out.

Having a social conscience didn't, though, slake my thirst for self-destruction. By the time I was sixteen I was off my head a lot of the time. I was being sucked into a cycle of decline almost without realizing it. The more I drank, the more I gravitated towards bad people and bad situations. What began with shoplifting and petty vandalism developed into drug arrests and illegal underage drink-driving.

I look back with a sense of shame, offset by relief that it could have been worse. We could so easily have killed the girl whose car we climbed into after one drinking binge. She lay down in the back seat, since she was so drunk she couldn't sit upright. I was in the passenger seat. A friend, off his face, got behind the wheel, and drove through a red light.

The car was T-boned, rolled three times, and came to rest in the bush on the other side of the road. I passed out on impact; when I came to I was hanging upside down between the two front seats. The girl was unconscious and covered in blood. Her head had taken the full force of the collision. She was rushed to hospital where, mercifully, she was diagnosed with severe concussion rather than anything immediately life-threatening.

We were arrested and taken to the cells. I escaped prosecution since I was not driving. My friend was charged and convicted, fined and sentenced to ten thousand hours of community service. The episode scared me rigid, but not enough to stop the stupidity.

Soon after, we were cruising around in the middle of the night, smoking dope, when we decided to stop in a park. We had got through a lot of Shiva, a particularly powerful strain of skunk, and hadn't noticed we were being followed by an unmarked police car. When the cops advanced towards us, guns drawn, I tried to throw the cannabis out of the car. I was so stoned I merely poured it over the seats, and into the footwell. One of the undercover cops opened the door, flashed his pistol in my face, and inhaled deeply. He recognized the pungent aroma and exclaimed, 'There's fucking Shiva all over the place.' Without pausing for breath, he dragged me out, slammed me down on the ground and read me my rights.

'What the fuck do you think you're doing?' he said. 'I almost shot you when I saw you duck down to try to clean up the mess. I thought you were reaching for a gun.'

It turned out we were in double jeopardy. They were acting on a tip-off that four black dudes, armed with automatic rifles, were in a similar car, casing houses to burgle. It transpired they were actually on the other side of the park, planning a break-in; the police reasoned, understandably enough, that we fitted the description of a bunch of criminals, up to no good.

'You don't know how lucky you are,' said another of the cops as he drove us to the police station, where we were banged up and charged with drugs offences. I was underage, so was allowed to leave, and one of the other parents dropped me off at home around 6 a.m. I was still insensible when Mum came downstairs, so my slurred explanation received short shrift. 'Fucking idiot,' she said, turning on her heels and walking away. I could not have argued against her, even if I'd had sufficient brain cells to do so.

Remarkably, I hadn't been excluded permanently from high school. At seventeen, in my final year, I winged my all-important matriculation examinations, photocopying notes made by a couple of the smart kids, and trying to cram nine months' work into two days' revision. Equally remarkably, I somehow passed six of the seven subjects for my National Senior Certificate.

I celebrated the only way I knew how, going on the piss, and tagging along with a couple of guys who were planning a gap year in the UK before university. We bummed around Scotland, doing agency work in factories and packaging plants, before cramming into a studio flat in Bristol, where we carried on drinking, smoking and fighting.

I was arrested after a massive punch-up in a nightclub which began when I laid out a guy who accused me of chatting up his girlfriend. The brawl ended up in the street; I had lost my shoes, my top had been ripped off, and I was fighting off a random stranger, who was trying to bite me. Just as the chaos subsided, I piled in again to help a mate, a really good rugby player who had tackled a bouncer in the solar plexus and was being battered for his pains. By the time we ended up in the police van we were in bits. For some bizarre reason, I've still got my arrest certificate, for being drunk and disorderly.

The highlight of the escapade came the following morning, when the observation slot in the cell door opened to reveal an officer, asking what I'd like for breakfast. I couldn't believe it. Beans, scrambled eggs, a slice of toast and a cup of tea. They'd also given me a blanket and a mattress to sleep off the session. I'd stayed in worse hotels and saw no reason to change my ways.

Packed off back to South Africa, I worked in an appropriately named bar called Shenanigans, where I distinguished myself by giving free pints to my mates.

Things were building to a head. I got into a scuffle with security guards in a shopping mall, where I leapt an ornamental fence and tried to steal a giant teddy bear, and found myself wandering aimlessly at 6 a.m. after a midweek cocaine binge. The tipping point came when Chris and I kicked the tail lights out of a BMW, parked in a driveway. We didn't see the driver, who gave chase as we sped off on a moped. Eventually he drove up the kerb, cut us off, and burst out of the car waving a pistol, screaming, 'I'm going to fucking kill you!' Looking at his wild eyes, as he held the gun to my head, I believed him.

Was this how it was going to end? With my lifeblood ebbing away on a darkened street as a random stranger took murderous revenge? What a waste. What a pathetic death.

I had reached the edge of darkness; but someone, somewhere, gave me a final chance that night. The driver's anger subsided. He relented, and returned silently to his car, but I knew, at that moment, that I couldn't continue as I was. If I stayed in Johannesburg I would end up in prison, or in the mortuary.

I needed to do something with my life. I needed something bigger than myself.

THREE

Bootneck

THE HARDEST THING about my paralysis is that it continually tests my faith. I am beyond the miracles of modern medicine, and will never walk again. It's almost impossible for my brain to compute. It's not as if I've a ten-year sentence to serve before earning my freedom. I could hack that. I know I will never get my former life back.

I've not given up, but the light at the end of my tunnel flickers and fades.

Before my injury my greatest pleasure involved identifying an ambition, relishing its difficulties, and immersing myself in achieving it, to the point of obsession. However distant and forbidding it felt, the goal drove me on, sucked me in, and gave me an ideal on which to focus. It enabled me to channel my misspent energies and save me from myself.

That was my thinking when I surprised everyone in South Africa by sharing my intention to become a Royal Marines Commando. The setting for my announcement, yet another bar on yet another pissy night out in Jo'burg, might have been predictable, but something fundamental had changed. I'd had enough of treading water with increasing desperation.

I was a mess. This was not what I was meant to be doing with my life. I had more to give, a destiny to fulfil. I thought I was meant for greater things. Reading about the Marines had seized my imagination. Those blokes were so tough, so gnarly, so hard core that no one in their right mind would give themselves a chance of proving themselves capable of joining them, as an equal.

Except that I did.

My mates tried, and failed, to talk me out of it. My brother Ben spent most of that night on his soapbox. 'Why are you going off to fight someone else's war?' he asked, reasonably enough. We were, after all, young and idealistic. 'You're going to get shot or blown up for someone else's politics.'

Despite everything that has happened since, he now understands my compulsion. He appreciates that the military gives guys a sense of discipline, authority and belonging, often at a trying time in their lives. In my case, he recognizes it was a perfect fit, a chance to purge myself with unspent passion. It was something I was probably born to do.

I had no conception what that would entail when I managed to rustle up enough money for the cheapest air ticket to London, and a basic bus journey to Bristol. I had no grand plan, other than to join the Corps. It was me, on my own, chasing a dream. I was going to stop at nothing until I achieved it.

I rented a room on a rundown estate, and stacked shelves in Tesco on the night shift, between 9 p.m. and 3.30 a.m., so that I could train during the day. I'd grab a couple of hours' kip, go down to the local park, pace out 100 metres, and do a series of sprints before pushing myself through a rough-and-ready circuit, consisting of press-ups and sit-ups.

Once I began to get a measure of my fitness, or relative lack of it, I would run into town and back, adding a couple of miles on a regular basis. I had only a pair of trainers, some rag-arse trackie bottoms and a couple of T-shirts, so wouldn't have fitted in at one of the leisure palaces in the more affluent areas. Instead, I saved enough for a basic contract at a council gym, which had a pool.

Exercise was good therapy. I'd swim in the mornings, run, and do weights in the evening, before going to work. Sitting in my room drove me insane, since I had no friends, and no one to talk to. To keep myself occupied, I would write poetry, song lyrics, and put fragments of memories down on paper. Don't ask me why, but I've always loved calligraphy. The flow of the lines and the flourish of the pen were hypnotic.

The folder containing my scribblings was, sadly, lost in transit, but the research I did, on the Royal Marines' heritage and traditions, stays with me. I'd heard it would form part of my interview, so I tried to cram in as many random facts as possible before I took a deep breath and headed for the Recruiting Centre. Here's a few, for your next pub quiz:

When were the Marines formed? On 28 October 1664, as the Duke of York and Albany's Maritime Regiment of Foot.

When did the Marines win their first three Victoria Crosses? In the Crimean War, 1854 and 1855.

In which operation did the Corps receive two VCs? Zeebrugge, April 1918: Captain Edward Bamford and Sergeant Norman Augustus Finch.

How many Commando battalions were raised during the Second World War? Nine.

I could go on, but I can hear you screaming for mercy. At least when I walked into the Recruiting Centre and announced my intentions to a squaddie who said 'Yeah, give me a second' before disappearing, I had an idea what would be asked of me. I understood the lifestyle to which I aspired. It was up to the sergeant major, who beckoned me to an upstairs office, to judge my character.

He drilled down into the reasons I was there, my interests and achievements. The background checks on my application were complicated because I hadn't lived in the UK for the requisite five years, but I was vetted through the South African embassy. When I received my letter of confirmation, detailing my orders to report for the PRMC – the Potential Royal Marines Course – I was elated.

I went back on the pints. For one day only.

I travelled light, by necessity. I stuffed a couple of pairs of socks, shorts and T-shirts along with some non-slip trainers into a battered backpack, and took the train to Exeter. Another four-carriage chugger took us around the mouth of the River Exe to the Marines training base at Lympstone. Forty of us reported for the four-day course. Around a quarter survived.

The first hurdle was a fitness test, in which we needed to score a minimum of sixteen points out of thirty. We had to reach at least level eleven on a 20-metre bleep test, and aim for sixty press-ups and eighty-five sit-ups in separate two-minute sessions. Muscles began to seriously scream when we were expected to perform at least eight controlled overhand pull-ups on a wooden beam.

A series of interactive lectures was subsequently followed by a 4.8-kilometre run, in two equal sections. The first had to be completed as a group in under twelve and a half minutes. The second, undertaken after sixty seconds' rest, was an individual exercise that had to be finished in less than eleven minutes and fifteen seconds. Then it was off to the pool, where we were obliged to dive from a 3-metre platform, swim 200 metres without pause in our kit, and retrieve a rubber brick from the bottom of the deep end.

A cosy chat with our corporal about the culture of the Corps brought the easiest full day of the course to an end. The thirty hours from dawn the following morning were a full-on beasting, which began with a test of nerve on the Tarzan Assault Course that involved climbing ladders, traversing ropes and negotiating obstacles up to 30 feet off the ground.

The bottom field at Lympstone belongs to the physical training instructors, the PTIs, hard men who can sniff out softness. They have devised a range of team exercises and personal challenges to weed out the weak, and reveal character flaws. The final full-scale physical test, lasting around ninety minutes and covering more than 2.5 miles of rough ground on Woodbury Common, some 4 miles away, does the rest.

More than a few are freaked out by claustrophobia, especially in the notorious sheep dip, a submerged tunnel that is the central feature of the endurance course. Instructors are looking for positivity and stamina when you are cold, wet and tired. They set the pace of your booted run back to the camp through the lanes in a hare and hounds exercise.

There's no respite. Equipment must be collected immediately, for an overnight exercise in what can be forbidding field conditions. Fitness, by this stage, is a given. Now you must work as part of a small team, to prepare food and shelter. Personal comfort is secondary to the protection of your equipment which, in other circumstances, could save your life.

I made it through, and was assigned to 926 Troop for the thirty-two-week basic training course. The scale of the opportunity meant I was almost bursting at the seams with excitement. I'd managed to reach the starting point. I was in the race. I had a massive point to prove to myself, and everyone else, that I was more than your average Joe.

Everyone is a little intimidated when they report. There were sixty-four of us, strangers slyly eyeing one another up to get an instant gauge of the strength of the competition. We were accommodated in a foundation block and assigned a metal-framed bed, a thin green mattress and a tall, relatively narrow brown cupboard.

It wasn't much, but it was home, for the first two weeks.

Modern recruitment slogans suggest being a Marine is 'a state of mind: you may already have it'. They have an initial impression of you, from the PRMC, and waste no time in probing behind the facade. They break you down and start to mould you from the first day, which involves taking the oath of allegiance and a shearing session with the camp barber.

Officially, training begins with 'housekeeping, etiquette and personal hygiene'. They may use the language of the Lucie Clayton Charm School, but any comparison is definitely coincidental.

Housekeeping involves getting up at 5.30 a.m., about three hours after you have finished ironing all your rigs, which must be folded A4 size and placed in your locker. Shirts must be hung precisely, and your two pairs of boots must be polished impeccably. Mess tins must sparkle and the weapons sling must be in perfect order. Woe betide

the recruit who pays insufficient attention to his BFA, which basically stops a live round accidentally coming out of the dangerous end
of the rifle.

By 6.30 a.m. you will have had a shit, shower and shave, and be
standing by your bed, which must be pristine, with hospital corners
and creases in all the right places. That's when you are introduced to
Corps etiquette, in the form of your drill leader, who proceeds to rip
you to shreds, even if everything is presented immaculately. Gear is
thrown all over the place, accompanied by a caustic commentary on
your inadequacy. Nothing is ever good enough, however good you
think you are. You know, from that moment, who is boss, and that
you are striving to reach the ultimate standards.

If you weren't in shock during the initial inspection, you probably
will be after your first lesson in personal hygiene, delivered in the
heads – communal toilets with a set of showers. In my case, the drill
leader stripped off and showed us how to wash. He scrubbed his
head, paid special attention to his underarms, and with the bellowed
reminder 'You will bend over' began scouring his arse and cleaning
his cock and balls. His party piece involved a recitation of the joys of
anal sex, followed by the flourish of pulling his foreskin back, to
reveal it had been smothered in Nutella.

You had to be there to appreciate the impact. I might have had
second thoughts on a chocolate spread sandwich in the galley later, but
knew I had found my place in the world. As I was reminded throughout training, this was my ticket to the ultimate boys' club. Others
couldn't wait to rip theirs up.

Blokes began leaving on the second day. Some were as young as
sixteen. It was their first time away from Mummy and Daddy and

you just knew they weren't going to make it. Pressure is applied instantly and doesn't ease. If you can't cope with the shouting and the ritual humiliations, you are not long for this world. It's a form of natural selection.

It's funny how human dynamics work. A sixth sense encourages stronger recruits to gravitate quickly towards one another. I hit it off immediately with John Knowles, who has become one of my closest mates. He was four years older than me, a five-year army veteran who had served in Northern Ireland before transferring on to the Corps programme. We bonded like brothers; we had similar upbringings, and shared a rebellious streak. By the end of the first week I had also formed lasting friendships with Wesley Grant, Dave Pink and Michael 'Taff' Francis. They, like John, were fantastic soldiers, though our troop stripy, Sergeant Kevin Roberts, known as 'Pedro' or 'Peds' due to his swarthy features, showed little sign of agreement.

He was hard as nails and came into our lives at the start of the third week, when we transferred to a training block, and billeted six to a room. He wasn't one for small talk, and did not care for the weak. 'You will cut the mustard or you will piss off,' he announced. 'There isn't an "i" in team but there definitely is a "u" in cunt and you're all cunts. You're useless fucking civvies.' He had adopted the persona of hating everyone, and was frighteningly authentic as a twenty-four-carat bastard. We were a grievance to him, a waste of his time. He consciously made our lives as difficult as possible, because we were worthless until we had earned our green lid – the Marines beret, complete with lion and crown badge that denotes a royal regiment.

Pedro was outranked only by our troop commander, a captain. He had four section commanders under him. The training team was completed by a drill instructor and a PTI. They took their lead from the sergeant: they were strict and unforgiving. By the end of the first phase of training, after sixteen weeks, only thirty-five of the original sixty-four recruits remained.

The process might have appeared brutal, but it was logical, and informed by current combat experience. All eight of our training team had recently returned from the front line. That allowed our instruction to be agile and adaptive. To give a specific example, our ambush drills were revised when the Taliban learned them on the battlefield, and set booby-traps in our best firing positions.

Equipment can also be upgraded quicker when it has been tested under fire. There's a natural cycle of progression, accelerated because in the Marines, and the SBS, responsibility is devolved down to the man on the ground to make decisions in a small, multi-disciplined team that operates on its own initiative.

In other ways, though, the Corps is wedded to history. Its vocabulary is insular and goes back hundreds of years. The nickname 'bootneck' for a Marine is derived from the leather cut from their boots and wrapped around their necks to prevent their throats being cut. This ensured their heads remained up, so they projected confidence and assurance. 'Scran' is food, 'oggin' is water. 'Gonk' or 'zeds' is slang for sleep, of which no trainee gets enough.

The regime is so relentless, there are times when it is impossible to keep your eyes open. That's why recruits are known as 'nods'. My moment of truth came during a weapons training lesson on the SA80, the standard British military rifle. The corporal was banging on about the importance of checking components, and wanted to be told why his demonstration model couldn't fire.

I was hanging out, nodding away, when I heard him say, 'Gutteridge, you're up first.' This was the alarm call from hell, since I hadn't listened to a word he'd said. He had a reputation for savagery, so I was forehead-deep in the shit. John Knowles, my so-called mate, was beside me. He hissed 'Sights, sights, Tobes, sights' and I duly parroted his version of the lecture.

Big mistake. The corporal went puce. 'What the fuck?' he exclaimed. 'I literally just said don't mention the sights.' He gave me an almighty bollocking and told me to drop to my belt buckle – shorthand for the prone position. He ordered me to leopard-crawl to the bottom field, submerge myself in the tank, which is full of slime and stagnant water, then leopard-crawl back to the weapons hut.

It took well over an hour to make it through the mud. I was filthy, exhausted, and smelled to high heaven. By that time the troop were on to their next drill. Knowlesy, of course, couldn't contain his glee when I caught up with them. Even to this day, when we get together he will whisper 'Sights, Tobes, don't forget the sights, mate' and start cackling.

Dick.

I'll admit, through gritted teeth, that we're very similar. We were as thick as thieves during training, causing havoc on runs ashore in Exmouth and Plymouth. I thought I could drink, but he once took me to the edge of oblivion on a two-week bender in Tenerife, which followed a Christmas break at his parents' house.

They lived on the rough side of Halifax. (To be honest, I'm not sure there's a posh side.) They were brilliant people who, knowing I had nowhere to go, welcomed me like a surrogate son to what was an alien world, in more ways than one. I'd never seen snow before that visit to Yorkshire. When we went out on an 8-mile morning run as a supposed hangover cure, I turned into a little kid, making snow angels and staging snowball fights.

John is a lovely soul. He takes excessive pride in the 'Made in Halifax' tattoo around his belly button, and continues to insist I should get a 'Made in Jo'burg' tattoo around mine. Absolutely no chance.

Predictably, when we returned from Tenerife to Lympstone we were jaded, to say the least. I'd put on about a stone and John smelled like a brewery. We were normally the best two trainees on the bottom field exercises; on the first test of the New Year we finished seventh and ninth respectively. We tried, and failed, to convince Pedro we were taking precautions to avoid peaking too early.

Marine humour is pretty dark and raw. Nothing – race, religion, gender and especially personal foibles – is off limits. If you have a sensitive nature, you are going to struggle to survive. A thick skin is essential, because they will keep probing until they find your pressure point, the chink in your chain. They'll nag away at that weakness until you snap.

It is a surreal process, funny as hell, and it keeps you grounded. It's an extension of the attitude of the training team. They dictate the pace and mood of your life throughout training. You learn to watch them, and notice how brutally they interact with one another. Their instinct is to take the piss first, and ask questions later.

They are in jackal mode in crash week, week nineteen, devoted to preparations for the critical four battle tests the following week.

They seek to push you to your physical limits, knowing that all tests are undertaken with full kit – at least 30lb of equipment. That didn't bother me: I felt strong and had just been awarded the PT medal, given to the troop's best performer in the gym.

By that time Knowlesy was operating as our section commander. I was his number two, the poor sap who would be roused from a light sleep and get out of bed at 2 a.m. to help him prepare for the day's principal tasks. I was a regular at the free supper, served at 9 p.m., so never got enough kip.

The battlefield tests begin with a 30-foot rope climb, timed passages across the assault course, and a 200-metre fireman's carry. That's followed by the pool test, which involves entering the water from the 10-metre board in boots and combat rig, and swimming 60 metres of breaststroke before removing your webbing and rifle. You are then expected to tread water for three minutes.

It was here that the legend of Sponge was born. He was a great guy, but not the greatest around water. He jumped in and sank like a stone, to the bottom of the pool. It took a few seconds before it became apparent that he wouldn't be surfacing of his own accord. Someone dived in, fished him out, and hauled him to the side. As he coughed and spluttered and regained his composure, an unseen voice piped up: 'Who do you think you are, mate? Fucking Spongebob Squarepants?' Everyone fell about, and the shortened version of his nickname stuck.

Speed marches, over 4, 6 and 9 miles, lead into the final examination of character, strength and resilience, a 12-mile load carry, involving 64lb of equipment, usually at night. Progress from that and you are into the Commando phase, which involves a lot of yomping, surveillance exercises, operational tactics and vertical assaults on strategic targets.

Only twelve of the original members of 926 Troop made it to the final tests, during week thirty-one. Wesley broke his ankle and was held back while he rehabbed. He remained with us in spirit; the bonds might have been unspoken, but they were unbreakable. This was where all the pain and persistence paid off.

It began with a 6-mile endurance course across rough moorland and woodland, through craggy gullies and wading pools in which the water can reach neck height. We negotiated 70 metres of tunnels and seven different obstacles, including an underwater culvert, the sheep dip, and the Smarties tube – a series of stone-floored tunnels that destroy the knees.

The kicker was the marksmanship exercise, undertaken after a 4-mile run back to base. To progress, we needed to hit six out of ten shots at a 25-metre target on the range. It is harder than it sounds, since you must control your fatigue, nerves, and the adrenaline rush of being confronted by the possibility of exclusion.

A 9-mile speed run over varying terrain tests teamwork, since you must begin the task as a troop, and end it intact. On the third test, the Tarzan Assault Course, it's every man for himself. This starts with the death slide, involves negotiating seven different obstacles at heights of up to 100 feet, and ends with a rope climb up a 30-foot near-vertical wall.

All that remains is the 30-miler, a speed march across Dartmoor whose origins can be traced back to the Second World War. It begins at Okehampton Battle Camp and involves carrying full fighting kit and additional safety equipment while negotiating roads, streams and bogs. The finish, across Shaugh Prior Bridge, which has strad-dled the River Plym since the seventeenth century, is imprinted in my brain.

Physically, you are shattered, spent. Emotionally, you are flying. There's a huge sense of personal and collective accomplishment. All twelve originals passed. This is a moment we will share until, one by one, we shuffle off this mortal coil. It will be our secret, revealed and revived by a glance.

Sergeant Kevin Roberts grasps your hand, looks you in the eye, and passes you your green beret.

'Congratulations. You are officially a Royal Marines Commando.'

It's one of the best days of your life.

The formalities are completed the following week, when you receive your cap, once again, from the camp commander, in a passing-out parade. That's a family occasion, though in my case my family didn't show up.

And it is here, in an ancient oak wood, beside a river littered with mossy boulders, where the walls come tumbling down. Pedro drops the pretence of professional disgust. The rest of the training team are ready to go on the lash with you. You start to see them as normal human beings. You can see the pride they take in your pride. They finally let on that they have seen something special in you. You are part of the team now. You are one of the brothers.

I love talking about those precious moments. It reminds me of a time in my life when I felt the real me.

Fate has subsequently intervened in different ways. I, at least, ful-filled my dream of making the Special Forces. Knowlesy, who could easily have made the next step, got close by joining the SF support group, but was not so fortunate. A routine examination discovered his hearing was so bad he had to be medically discharged.

We had the choice of joining one of four battalion-sized subordinate units. 42 Commando were based at Bickleigh Barracks, near Plymouth, 43 Commando were assigned the Faslane nuclear base, and 45 Commando were situated in Arbroath. Dave Pink and two other guys to whom we'd become close during training, Aidan Heyworth and Andrew Starkey, joined me in 40 Commando at Norton Manor Camp in Taunton.

We were known as the sunshine boys. It was a lovely place, but my choice wasn't down to the impression it would be all flip-flops and factor fifty. I'd done my homework. 40 Commando were scheduled as the next unit to be deployed to Afghanistan, in October 2007.

I had six months to prepare myself for battle.

FOUR

Under Fire

I DIDN'T JOIN the Royal Marines to become a chef, a mechanic or a stores accountant. I signed up because I wanted to go to war. It was a unique chance to live on the edge and experience extremes beyond the comprehension of most people. This may seem incredibly naive, or dangerously trite, but I really wanted to make a difference.

To what, or who, I'm still not sure. There was an element of the five-year-old me proving myself to my stepdad, by sharing his first-hand knowledge of combat. The bonds of the military brotherhood, a basic attraction, would tighten over time and under fire, but big-picture politics and notions of duty to a higher cause barely registered.

I've no intention of glorifying violence, but the more I think about it, I was following a primal instinct. Theories that man is predisposed to fighting seem to be backed up by behavioural scientists, whose research suggests human beings are six times more likely to kill one of their own species than the average mammal.

If you read the self-help books, the traits of an alpha male are assumed to be complementary, and occasionally contradictory. Courage is matched by control. Awareness of strength is balanced by an acceptance of weakness. He feels no need to explain, but there's a compulsion to say what is on his mind. Instant decisions and strategic planning can dovetail.

Such assumptions are nice and neat, but life is messy.

I was in an alpha male environment, where self-belief often manifested itself as bravado. Testosterone lingered in the air like a teenager's first aftershave, pungent and faintly fruity. A lot of the guys were trying to prove something; I wasn't sure whether that was to themselves, or others. I simply needed to know that I had what it takes.

Reckon you're a macho man? Put yourself in my position, during initial pre-deployment exercises. It's one thing to go through the basics of medical training, such as how to put a tourniquet on. It's entirely another to trust a hairy-arsed Marine coming towards you with a three-inch needle with the intention of practising running a line into an artery. OK, he's a mate. But you know, and he's all too aware, that he's never done anything like this in his life. He's shaking like a leaf, which isn't the best bedside manner, especially when you are alone in the bush. He might sneakily watch a bit of *Holby City* when he is at home on leave, but inserting a cannula is pretty alien to him. You've both got no option but to submit to the process.

That's the essence of preparing to go to war. Salisbury Plain is no one's idea of the Sangin Valley, but it was the best place we had to recreate the sort of patrols we would be expected to conduct and the operational challenges we'd have to face. We drilled incessantly, and repeated specific scenarios, so that when the time came, instinct had a better chance of kicking in.

Familiarization lectures gave us the lie of the land, and enabled us to visualize what enemy compounds would look like. Physical fitness was a given, but still checked regularly. We began to accumulate kit.

It took simulation exercises, conducted by directing staff who had just come back from a tour of duty, to make it all seem real. When a DS pulled you up and told you that you had made a mistake that would have been fatal in battle, your blood ran cold.

Shit. That's me killed. There will be no second chances in Afghan.

They weren't trying to scare you with horror stories, but they did make you think. This, remember, was around the time the Paras were getting decimated. Other army regiments were taking mass casualties. We had every incentive to pick the brains of those who had seen the human cost of an ugly guerrilla war.

They warned, time and again, about the threat of IEDs. Lives and limbs were being lost. Sangin, our most obvious point of assignment, was referred to as 'a low-density minefield'. The Taliban were becoming increasingly subtle in their deployment of roadside bombs; suicide bombers were a greater menace than one-on-one firefights, which were increasingly rare.

The messages were stark, and taken to heart. Trust no one when you are out on patrol, however placid or friendly they may appear. Look after your mates, your six. Be very cautious, because it only takes someone to let their guard slip for a split second for things to go very wrong, very quickly. You have no idea what's around the next corner.

They tried to teach us how to identify insurgents, which to be honest is practically impossible. We were shown specific tattoos, worn on the hand or wrist, but I never saw any evidence of them. A farmer who picks up an AK-47 doesn't announce himself with name, rank and serial number. In practical terms, learning key words and phrases in the primary national language, Pashto, proved far more valuable.

Our schoolboy errors in training tended to be tactical decisions that weren't thought through properly. A common one was to unwittingly take the wrong route, typically through a gorge, and allow the enemy, positioned on high ground, to channel your patrol into an ambush or a mined area. Another involved being careless around main entrances to compounds, which tended to be booby-trapped and heavily defended during an assault.

Did it put me off? Hand on heart, no. You never think it is going to happen to you, do you?

It does seep into the subconscious, though. You have dreams about going into combat. That's understandable, since the prospect pretty much fills every waking hour. The Marines do nothing by accident. Training is designed to foster a sense of pride, and to get you into the right frame of mind to enter a battle zone.

It is drilled into you that you represent the best of the best. The Paras are phenomenal, and some of the other army units are fantastic, but you are better than all of them. You're the ultimate warrior, ready to confront whatever the world chooses to throw at you. In a sense, the truth is of marginal importance. If you believe you deserve top billing, that's all that matters.

Nothing, of course, prepares you for the moment you fly into Camp Bastion. The atmosphere on the C-17 Globemaster flight from the UK is surprisingly light-hearted but the mood changes when all aircraft lights are switched off, prior to landing. It's a reminder that you are, literally, a sitting target. In the darkness, hearts pound, and everyone tries to come to terms with a new reality.

What am I doing here? There's no turning back now. This is it. Here we go.

The dry heat hits you as you disembark, and the sense of normality, as you are directed into a massive hangar that houses a miniature passport control, is surreal. It's all very civilized and conventional, but completely out of context. I didn't expect to run off the Boeing to find the bloody Taliban charging at me, but having my passport stamped, as if I was a tourist, wasn't on my radar.

The camp was pretty much in the middle of nowhere, a desert location north-west of the city of Lashkar Gah in Helmand Province. Its scale, 4 miles long and 2 miles wide, was difficult to take in, though it felt as if I knew every yard because of the perimeter runs on which we had gauged our fitness. It had grown from a few tents in 2005 to a base for up to twelve thousand soldiers by the time we arrived on 10 October 2007.

It feels strange to think of it now as a relic of military history, but Bastion was capable of accommodating thirty-two thousand people when it was handed over to the Afghan army at the end of October 2014. A conflict that wrecked or ended the lives of so many good men became an afterthought that occasionally re-emerged in the small print of newspapers until the Taliban seized control of the country in the late summer of 2021.

Progress? I'll leave that to you to decide. It's a painful subject to which I will return later in the book.

My troop – 1 Troop, Alpha Company, 40 Commando – slept thirty to a tent during a two-week transitional period. For the first time I was under orders to wear my two dog tags around my neck at all times. They featured my name, service number, blood group (A minus) and my religion. Why two tags? That represented yet another reality check.

One would be pulled off, as a means of identification, if I died in combat. The other would be left on the body, to complete the process. If they were lost, I could be tracked down by my Zap number, G077N, which consisted of the first letter of my surname and the last four digits of my service number. This could be found on a badge on my chestplate.

All that remained, essentially, was to discover our area of operation. Bravo Company were assigned to the village of Sangin, north-east of Bastion; Charlie Company rocked up at the Kajaki Dam, about 20 miles further up on the Helmand River; and Delta Company were directed to a forward operating base (FOB) along the valley. Those of us in Alpha Company took an hour's Chinook flight from Bastion to FOB Inkerman, situated 6 miles north-east of Sangin.

The holiday brochures weren't exactly alluring. Inkerman was commonly referred to as FOB Incoming. It was bombarded constantly by missiles, mortars and Chinese-made rockets. It measured around 300 metres in length and consisted of two heavy metal doors, four compound walls, a few mud huts, the odd container and some desultory, dusty tents.

We relieved lads from the First Battalion, the Grenadier Guards, and C Company, from the First Battalion of the Royal Anglians. They had been there for more than six months and were on the bones of their arses. They were sitting on empty ammunition tins, in absolute rag order. Their faces were caked with dirt because there were no washing facilities. Their beards were wild and wiry. Their hair had been matted into dreadlocks by sweat and dust. They had been sleeping on the floor, as best they could, and looked like a bunch of castaways. They had taken heavy casualties and you could see, in their eyes, that they were traumatized. They did their best to share operational details, the optimal routes in and out of the compound; they gave us an insight into the nature and timing of Taliban attacks. But they couldn't wait to get the hell out of there.

Best of luck, guys. Jesus, you'll need it. Just stay away from the high points in the compound, stay away from the corners, and pray there's not a missile with your name on it.

We all knew, from that moment, this would be full on. Would we be in their state when we completed our tour the following April? How many of us would survive?

This wasn't a Vietnam War movie, but it certainly felt like one. I'd watched *Platoon* as a kid and never, in my wildest dreams, thought I'd experience it for real.

The setting, overlooking the green belt on the high ground of the valley, was as bleak as our mood. Irrigation ditches, branching off the main river and meandering down the valley, screamed danger. Mud-walled buildings were strewn randomly across poppy fields that seemed to stretch for ever. The plants were mid-thigh high, with seed pods, which turned brown as they dried, on top of long stems.

You didn't need to be a pharmacologist or a political activist to read between the lines of why you were there. The fields represented economic insurance during the global financial crash of 2007/08. War is another way of driving income and investment. Western-backed campaigns to eliminate poppy cultivation or to encourage farmers to grow other crops were futile. Before everyone knew it, Afghanistan had become the supplier of 90 per cent of the world's opium. Revenues from certain areas of the country were being recycled to fund the insurgency. Sangin was a pinch point for the region's drug trade. Local leaders, at the centre of a complex web of shifting allegiances, looked after number one.

We were fighting spectres, shadows. If the mood took them, today's farmers, tending their crops, would return as tomorrow's fighters. They had families to feed, a subsistence living to make. It was impossible to ignore the resentment in their stares, but contempt was tinged with confusion. It was as if they didn't really understand why we were there.

The tribal elders had lived their entire lives in a war zone. They had been invaded regularly since the Russians turned up in the early eighties. The land was scarred and cratered. Buildings were peppered with holes. To them, this was same shit, different flag. They were sick of death and destruction. They didn't care about political or cultural philosophies. They just wanted us to piss off.

I was just twenty-two. If roles were reversed would I, as a twenty-two-year-old Afghan, fight the Brits? Honestly? Absolutely.

They grew up fast and died young. Child militia were common. Kids were used as human shields, as part of a defence strategy. Some became suicide bombers. When on patrol you'd be more scared of children than anyone else, especially if they were employed in what looked like everyday activities such as pushing a wheelbarrow. The mundane sight of a barrow piled with logs was menacing. Kids had been known to wheel their load towards troops before detonating plastic explosives packed beneath the wood, killing themselves and anyone they could take with them. How can you prepare yourself for something like that? It is mind-boggling to conceive and impossible to get used to.

It's difficult enough to cope with, psychologically, when you are fit and well. When you are suffering from the sort of outbreak of vomiting and diarrhoea that laid low a third of our company in the early weeks of our tour, it is horrendous. Blokes were throwing up and crapping everywhere, because they didn't have the time or energy to reach black bins set up for the purpose in a ditch. We had nowhere to wash our hands, so you can imagine how fast disease spread. You'd hear people retching throughout the night, and know they'd be in the med bay by morning.

The term 'med bay' may conjure visions of a smart field hospital. This was a twelve-man canvas tent which was overrun. Blokes were lying about on stretchers in whatever shade we could find for them. For all the trillions of dollars spent on military hardware, in many ways we were closer to the soldier of 1807 than the technologically enabled fighter of 2007.

It generally took seven days to recover, but quite a few guys had to be evacuated to Bastion because their dehydration was life-threatening. We had no fresh water and were completely cut off until the supply helicopter arrived, at dusk or dawn, throwing off anti-missile flares. The medics were brilliant, but when you are sleeping on the ground and shitting in a ditch, what can you do?

Since we were struggling to put out patrols, our ranks were bolstered by the Gurkhas. They were good people, practical, brave and resourceful. One managed to negotiate with the locals for a goat, which they slaughtered and made into a stew. To those of us existing on ten-man ration packs, it was a taste of heaven.

Hell lay outside the metal doors of the compound, through the poppy fields, along ditches, ravines and dirt roads. Things were ratcheting up. Within a year, it was estimated the Taliban had planted 1,200 bombs in one square kilometre in Sangin, some within 30 metres of British outposts. Most of their ordnance was scavenged from the Soviets in the eighties.

Your senses are instantly heightened when an IED detonates. The noise becomes familiar. You visualize the deadly hail of scrap metal, nuts, bolts, pieces of tin and stones. You feel the blast wave, the pressure that disturbs the dust. You hear radios, radiating urgency: 'Casualties, casualties ... shots fired, shots fired ... crossfire ... enemy seen ...' You wonder, for a split second, who has copped it, and pray it is not one of your mates.

Our first contact with the insurgents came when a lad in our recce troop was fragged – our slang for being blown up. He was in a pretty bad way. The fronts of both his legs were terribly damaged, though surgeons subsequently managed to avoid amputation. Another lad was shot in the upper chest during the chaos of calling in support, organizing an evacuation, and returning fire.

You have no option but to deal with the stress, but in a way you never get used to doing so. Your heart rate goes through the roof. There's a fleeting shortness of breath. You are trying to think clearly, remember your drills and the minutiae of what you have been taught. You are not thinking, 'There's the Taliban – let's get them.' It's more about keeping your mates safe.

My job was to help secure a landing site for the rescue helicopter. This involved moving quickly and decisively to cordon off a poppy field, despite the ever-present threat of mines and heavy incoming fire. A couple of mates were on the portable 51mm mortar, pinning the enemy back as best they could, while I laid down fire with a heavy machine gun.

We were firing at vague noises, looking for impressions of movement and listening for the differences between incoming and outgoing fire. When you hear the crack of a rifle, followed by the bull-whip snap of bullets breaking the sound barrier just above your head, you know you are under fire from close range. Rounds ping off rocks, walls, and make the ground dance.

While this was going on, the section commander sought orders from base. The JTAC (joint terminal attack controller) gave coordinates to mortar crews back at Inkerman, and the FAC (forward air controller) called in air support from A-10 Thunderbolts, which basically shoot the shit out of everything during a series of low-flying passes.

The rescue helicopter pilot initially radioed in that it was too hot to land, but quickly reversed the call, and came in under heavy fire. These guys are fantastic; amazingly brave and remarkably skilful, they do their utmost to get the lads out, whatever the personal risk. Once they landed, the doctor had to pick his moment to leap out, because the attack was so intense.

No one truly knows how they will deal with overwhelming fear, when the occasion arises. We had managed to get the casualties to the site and were liaising with the medic on the ground, who had plugged wounds and stopped the bleeding, when one of our interpreters, who had given himself the nickname The Rock, tried to force his way on to the helicopter. Such civilians were invaluable, and I feel a genuine sense of pride that many were allowed to settle in the UK when the conflict initially subsided, because their service put their lives at risk. He was terrified, in the sort of panic that gets people killed. How many would-be rescuers have been drowned by the flailing swimmer they were trying to save? Since he was running around like a headless chicken and beyond listening to reason we knocked him out and explained why later. It would be a couple of years before I learned his fate. He stepped on an IED during a subsequent tour, and was killed instantly.

May he rest in peace. He was another victim of circumstance, in an enduring human catastrophe; another tragedy, buried beneath the sands of time.

Our priority, that blisteringly hot afternoon, was to get our casualties out of harm's way. That involved four of us bearing them into the helo on an emergency stretcher. This was done on the run, after a two, six lift that supposedly dates back to the earliest days of the Marines and the manning of shipboard cannon. The theory went that the team of six men on the ropes had numbered roles; after loading, the gunners numbered two and six had to heave the cannon out of the gunport in a synchronized manner for firing.

To be brutally honest, history didn't seem terribly relevant at the time.

Once the lads were safely evacuated, the priority changed. Break contact with the enemy, and retreat to base as fast as possible. It wasn't that simple, of course. The Taliban knew we were hot, tired and thirsty. They had been monitoring us from the moment we emerged from the FOB that morning.

We knew what was up, since we intercepted radio transmissions from a so-called dicker, reporting our movements to the insurgent commander. I had seen a few guys who looked mega sketchy, staring at us intently as we passed. They wore black turbans and were newly shaved – a tell-tale sign of preparation for martyrdom.

What could we do? Nothing until it all kicked off.

It was a couple of kilometres back to base. We had trained continually in the disciplines of retreat, but rehearsal offers the safety blanket of a lack of real jeopardy. When you are being pushed back, running with heavy equipment and looking after yet another casualty, your mind and body are fighting against you.

Anarchy is breaking out all around. Mortars, fired from cannons at the FOB, are landing. You can only pray their aim is true. Low-flying planes are strafing areas of enemy activity. You are exchanging fire, looking for the flash of a muzzle or even a head popping up somewhere. It's like a movie set. One part of your brain is questioning whether it is real. Another is trying to control your fear.

Have they planned an ambush? Are there snipers in that hut in the distance? What other firing positions do we have to look out for? Where are the rest of our blokes?

You're listening for their warnings and instructions, because a lack of communication is dangerous. It is easy to become confused in such a frenzied situation. The last thing you want to do is lose your bearings and mistakenly start shooting in the wrong direction, at other sections. Blue on blue casualties are your worst nightmare.

We were getting slammed, but there was no thought of inflicting casualties. We had no advantage in outright attack, and concentrated on laying down covering fire over a distance of a couple of hundred metres. Nerves were shredded. Physically, we had reached our limits. It took two hours before the metal doors of Inkerman opened, and we found refuge.

There was no elation, only exhaustion. Blokes were lying where they fell, trying to catch their breath. You could see they were on the edge, emotionally. There was so much to process, and make sense of. You didn't know whether to laugh or cry that you'd made it back to base. You didn't know whether you were coming or going.

You are still on maximum alert. Your breathing sounds super loud. Your eyes flicker, trying to take in who is around you. You can see things so clearly. You are on sensory overload. Your brain is working at a thousand miles an hour. It feels like a near-death experience, and it takes you a long time to come down from it.

As I gained greater experience, became a bit more battle wise, I got better at channelling my emotion. But that night seemed endless. We had a mass debrief and went back to our designated areas before getting together for dinner. We didn't really have conversations; we simply shared streams of consciousness.

Sleep was impossible. Blokes were wired. It was as if we were all on drugs.

The next day brought a fleeting sense of perspective before the shelling started again. We had a day's grace from patrolling, but the moment we heard the shrill whistle of an incoming rocket we scattered like ants, diving towards any cover we could find. We were living in a series of roofless bays, so were prisoners of fate. Protection was minimal.

Rockets were being launched from rooftops, or from behind nearby buildings. They took out one of our sentry towers, and were landing about 10 metres away from where we were supposed to sleep. Some came over the walls, embedded themselves and failed to explode. Another problem that we didn't need.

Deep down, we knew what was coming. And when death comes calling, and takes someone close to you, it pierces your heart.

FIVE

Big Dee

From: Ministry of Defence

Field of operation: Afghanistan

It is with great sadness that the Ministry of Defence must confirm the death of Corporal Damian Mulvihill of 40 Commando Royal Marines yesterday, Wednesday 20 February 2008, in Helmand Province, Afghanistan.

Shortly before 1215 hrs local time Corporal Mulvihill was taking part in a joint ISAF-ANA patrol engaged in operations near Sangin. The Marines of Alpha Company were conducting a clearance patrol to deter Taliban intimidation of local Afghans. It was during this action that an Improvised Explosive Device was detonated, which sadly killed Corporal Mulvihill instantly. He died leading his section and the Company from the front.

Corporal Damian 'Dee' Mulvihill was born on 5 June 1975 and was from Plymouth. He joined the Royal Marines on 20 September 1998 and completed Commando training despite contracting septicaemia towards the end. After passing out of recruit training, 'Dee' joined 42 Commando Royal Marines where he took part in numerous deployments around the world as well as taking part in OP PALLISER and OP SILKMAN in Sierra Leone and OP BANNER in Northern Ireland.

During his time at 42 Commando he was promoted to Lance Corporal. He then joined Air Defence Troop in 2002 and completed his specialist training before being promoted to Corporal in December 2003. On completion of his service with the United Kingdom Landing Force Command Support Group, based at Stonehouse Barracks in his home town of Plymouth, he joined Alpha Company, 40 Commando Royal Marines in April 2006.

'Dee' was a giant of a man who impressed all who met him. Ever cheerful, he would never allow problems to get him down. He always had a friendly word for anyone he met and his fantastic personality filled any room he walked into. He was an excellent listener and would always make time for others.

'Dee' loved his boxing and rugby and represented the Royal Marines at rugby union. He was also a keen water polo player and represented the Royal Navy and the Combined Services team at the sport. 'Dee' was a true character who will be fondly remembered by all who had the privilege to serve with him. Humorous, caring and a true friend, he will be sadly missed by all his comrades in 40 Commando Royal Marines and the wider Corps family.

'Dee' leaves behind a loving fiancée, Lisa, and family of whom he talked about lovingly to anybody and everybody. He and Lisa were planning to get married in the near future, and our deepest sympathies are extended to Lisa, his parents and all family and friends.

Damian's family and Lisa have asked for the following statement to be released on their behalf:

'He was so loved by the whole family. He never had a bad word to say about anyone and always looked for the good in people. He was a son, a brother and uncle in a million, and a soul-mate to Lisa, and we will all miss him for ever. From Mum, Dad, Claire, Sam, and Lisa.'

A thousand mourners attended the big man's funeral, with full military honours, in his home city, Plymouth. Even after all these years, I can close my eyes and see every contour of his open, smiling face. I'm able to sense his calmness, and feel the strength of the grip he exerted, with hands like shovels. It doesn't take long for sadness to overwhelm fondness, but for those few seconds Big Dee returns to life. His spirit is set free.

When a mate dies on an operation it goes deep. You tell yourself, 'This isn't really happening. It can't be true.' It is a wilful act of self-delusion. You instinctively remember the last time you spoke, the laughs you had, the plans you shared about a future he will never experience. He's gone. You can't rewind time. You're helpless.

The eeriness of death stays with you.

We all develop a relationship with death, as we go through life. The loss of a childhood pet introduces us to grief. The passing of a parent is a rite of passage during adulthood. Friends contract terminal diseases. It is an inevitable interaction. We even experience it vicariously, by reading about, or watching, disasters, tragedies and wars in places we could not find on a map.

Losing Dee felt different, because it was so undeserved. His sacrifice was so hard to comprehend. It left you consumed by anger and frustration, but you can't get your head around who, or what, you are angry with. Are you raging at life itself, or at the person who cold-bloodedly waited before detonating the bomb as Dee's Viking passed over it?

The Taliban were targeting higher ranks. Their methods, incorporating the use of pressure pads, trip wires, radio waves or mobile phone signals, were increasingly sophisticated. The vertical force of the explosion punched a hole through the armour plating underneath Dee's all-terrain vehicle. He didn't stand a chance. My anger was laced with guilt that I was not on patrol with him.

I had been granted my requisite two weeks' R&R in the UK. I tried, and failed, to talk my way out of it, because I knew I would be sitting on my arse at 40 Commando's base in Taunton, since I had no family to visit. The camp was more or less deserted. One of the guys minding the shop came to my grots – my accommodation – to tell me the news.

It really messed with my head. I loved Dee. He was my section commander, a fantastic guy. I reverted to type, went on a bender and got absolutely ring-bolted. I didn't need a posse to share my misery. I drank on my own, initially in a squaddie bar called the Airport Lounge and then at a nightclub called Shout.

By 3 a.m. I had completely lost it. I was acting the loudmouth, saying inappropriate things about the nature of Dee's death and raging at bouncers trying to usher me out of the club. A couple of guys who had just called it a night came up to me and tried to calm me down: 'Hey, man, we've all been there. Just keep it down.'

I was idiot drunk: 'What the fuck are you talking about? You don't know shit.'

They tried to talk me down, but when it became apparent I was out of control they took me round the back of the club and filled me in. It was a real good shoeing. I tried to fight back but I was so pissed I could not have fought my way out of a paper bag. They left me lying in a pool of blood with a black eye, extensive facial cuts and a huge weal across my forehead.

I was found by a mate, who quickly discovered they were a pair of Special Forces guys based in Poole who lived in the area. They were obviously mega experienced, guys who were continually on operations. I was a sprog on my first tour, chopsing off and making a scene. It was their way of telling me that I was a Royal Marines Commando, and this was not how you behaved.

They gave me a life lesson in how to conduct myself that night. I'm grateful for it. I really am, because I deserved it. I acted like a child and they showed me the error of my ways in short, sharp order. I felt embarrassed the next day. I never found out who they were, though I made enquiries. If by any chance you're reading this, thank you.

They taught me something, which registered deep inside. I was young, immature, and didn't know how to deal with death. It was not until after my injury that I started to discuss the circumstances and implications of Dee's loss with my psychotherapist Ross Hoar, who specializes in trauma, PTSD and addictions. I began to understand the power of personal experience.

Most of the death I've encountered has been horrific. Growing up in South Africa I became accustomed to urban violence, deadly hijackings, random murders and senseless slaughter when robberies went wrong. My stepdad closed down all talk of combat casualties when I tried to raise it with him: left to my own devices, my imagination ran riot. I assumed my end would be horrendous, and became fearful of it.

My mindset only changed when Ross challenged me, in that measured, reasonable way he has: 'Have you ever seen anyone die peacefully in their bed, surrounded by their family? They're happy to go. It's actually a very beautiful thing.' That shook me to the core. I was like 'No, what?' My relationship with death was that it was inevitably going to be a terrible ordeal. I knew everyone had to face it at some point, but it was only by talking to a professional that I realized it doesn't have to be hideous. Without knowing it, I had undergone informal trauma training.

I'm not sure this entirely makes sense, but the act of reminiscence is healing. I now prefer to dwell on softer memories of Dee. He was like an older brother, easy to talk to and non-judgemental. He saw that I was very green, but that I had the foundations to make a very good soldier. He understood I was hungry to learn.

I was always asking questions about his role as a corporal, and how the military pecking order worked. I had ideas beyond my pay grade. Other people would get fed up with me, but he recognized that I had a drive to do better. He gave me his time and happily slaked my thirst for knowledge. He sensed the self-discipline that was to come.

He was such a placid character, nothing fazed him. He was one of those guys you see in operational zones who are battle-hardened. They are calm and collected. They just know the score. Inside, they're on edge as much as the next man, but externally, they're chilled. They sit around, in a compound where there's no aerial cover and they're pro-tected from the sun by a few bits of tarpaulin, radiating reassurance.

Thinking of Dee, I'm back in that fort, smelling the dust which scoured our throats. I'm reliving a patrol along the Sangin River, about three months into the tour. It was a good time, for want of a better word. We came under fire, were pinned down for a while, and reached the tipping point where it was impossible to get back to the FOB before sunset.

We didn't do night ops, because they were too risky. The odds on standing on something in the darkness were too high. We were freezing, starving and thirsty, yet had no option but to take shelter in a disused compound. Amazingly, one of the lads had brought his jet boily (a small gas cooker) along with him. He had one sachet of tea, and just enough water to fill a cup. It was decided that all thirty of us on the patrol would share the tea, one sip each.

While some of the section tried to snatch some sleep, I took my turn to freeze my tits off on an hour's sentry duty. When I was relieved I walked straight in and kicked the tea, which had just boiled after a painstaking wait, all across the dirt floor.

That tea was liquid morale.

It took a fraction of a second for the shock to register before I had every insult in the book thrown at me. The mildest and certainly most original piece of abuse referred to me as 'a fucking piece of rhino shit'. I had never wanted the ground to swallow me up so badly. There was no salvaging it; I just had to take the stick on the four-hour retreat to base the following morning.

Even those who wanted to throttle me – and they were in the majority – eventually laughed about it. The brotherhood was tight, really tight. They soon cottoned on to the fact I wasn't receiving any letters or parcels from home. They knew the value of a 'bluey', a note from a loved one, and relished the arrival of treats on the resupplying

Chinook. The lads would get boxes of chocolates, biscuits and little luxuries like a can of deodorant. When I told them I had no one to write to, they decided it was out of order. They chipped in behind my back, and asked their families to send an extra parcel for me. Before I knew it I had more treats than anyone. Their relatives would write me letters, asking after me and telling me to keep safe.

I get emotional every time I'm reminded of the gesture. It was so special. We looked after one another, and still do. Most of the guys have left the military. Fate has been kinder to some than others. It becomes progressively more complicated, but we try to meet annually, and communicate through an online group chat.

When we were out on patrol we relied on one another. The safest way to move was in single file, with a couple of metres between us, along a trail cleared by a point man with a mine detector. We walked in the footprints of the bloke in front, and kept a sharp eye out for disturbed soil. If it was a darker brown it meant it had probably been recently dug. Far safer to step on hard, compacted sand.

Negotiating the poppy fields was a nightmare. We'd try to use paths worn down by the locals, but when we came under fire we had no choice but to take our chances and dive for cover. I'd seen the extent of IED injuries, lads returning home as double or even triple amputees, but the alternative, being shot at relatively close range, also didn't bear thinking about.

There were anti-personnel mines everywhere. We found bar mines fully 6 feet long, virtual planks of plastic explosive. We even discovered an old Russian 500lb bomb under a bridge. In those circumstances, you took your lead from your seniors. Dee looked after each and every one of us.

He was a huge dude, but wasn't aggressive in any way, shape or form. We spent a lot of time together on sentry duty in our rudimentary watch tower at Inkerman, bonding initially over a shared love of sport in general and rugby in particular. South Africa's win over England in the 2007 Rugby World Cup final a couple of weeks after we had deployed gave me temporary bragging rights.

He also excelled at water polo, which was a huge sport in my teenage years. Those guys were super fit. They trained from 4 a.m., returned to the pool at lunchtime to swim another 2.5 kilometres, and completed a strength session in the evening by treading water for hours. I saw a friend of mine, who represented South Africa at Under-21 level, do that while holding a couple of 2-litre bottles of Coca-Cola, filled with water, over his head.

Night watches were a time of reflection and revelation. We found it easy to talk to each other, because Afghanistan was, literally, our common ground. We had become attuned to the environment, but knew there was nothing remotely normal about being shelled every day, or shitting in a bucket in the corner of the compound, and burning it.

Dust – brown and powdery when dry, cloying mud or slush in winter – was a constant source of annoyance. These were far from First World War levels of squalor, but it is unnatural for a human being to exist in such conditions for long periods of time. The walls came tumbling down, metaphorically, around 2.30 a.m., when we were at our lowest ebb, physically and psychologically.

I opened up to Dee about my struggles growing up, and my search for meaning. I tried to explain the gnawing feeling of being an outsider, and the impact that private sense of isolation had on my determination to better myself. He was ten years older, much more mature, and seemed closer to finding answers to life's biggest questions.

We talked a lot about why we had chosen the military as a career, and what that said about us as people. He considered himself a lifer. He wanted to stay in the Corps, do his twenty-two years, and get his pension. He had done a lot of thinking during his fortnight's R&R, and had put feelers out about moving on to Lympstone as a drill leader.

Being part of a training team worked both ways for him. It would have enabled him to share his knowledge in a meaningful way, in an atmosphere he loved. It would also have offered him a degree of stability and security. He planned to marry Lisa, his soulmate, and settle down.

He would have been brilliant at weeding out the small minority of flaky characters who join up for the wrong reasons. They tend to find it easy to put on a facade, and take advantage of the fact the Corps is looking for someone who is not afraid to go in there and do the job. They occasionally slip through the net, and their faults do not become apparent until it is almost too late.

You can't be a dog on a leash that must never be relaxed, for fear of the consequences.

The Marines attracts tough buggers from tough backgrounds. Many are fiercely patriotic and want to serve their country with every fibre of their being. Others, like me, are more nuanced. They're not there for the cause, though they are extremely loyal. They have an inquisitive nature that's not satisfied by the nine-to-five. They want powerful experiences, searing memories.

Dee was the first person I told of my determination to make it into the Special Forces. On the face of it, it was a hugely unrealistic ambition. I was a kid in my first year, on my first tour. Convention demanded that, even to be accepted into the elite group on the selection process, I needed to have two tours and at least six years under my belt.

Yet he simply said: 'You'd be an ideal candidate. I'll support you.'

That's why he left such a huge void. The mood at Inkerman, after his body had been repatriated following a dignified, gut-wrenching ceremony on the tarmac at Bastion, was sombre. There was an unnerving quietness about the place. Guys were keeping themselves to themselves. Morale was low.

It was a collective trauma, with individual consequences. A mate of mine, known to all as Mudders, was sitting directly behind Dee at the time of the explosion. Trapped in the twisted remains of the vehicle, he had the hopeless, horrible task of feeling for a pulse. I could only imagine what that was like. It properly messed him up; all I could do was be there for him.

The last high-profile job we did under Dee was Operation Snakepit, the retaking of Musa Qala, alongside the Americans and other members of the multi-national task force. Our role was to provide a show of force on the outskirts of town, confuse the insurgents with the unpredictability of our actions, and disrupt their supply routes. We had a company of Vikings and Mastiffs, which we slept under when we were not dug in, as part of a contingent of two thousand British troops that advanced from the south, west and east. We set up a cordon around the town to assist the main strategic assault by US troops, who were airlifted to the north in nineteen helicopters.

The Americans meant business. The horizon at night was illuminated consistently by long white flashes of light, followed, a couple of seconds later, by the familiar thud of distant explosions.

We came into regular contact with the Taliban – a strangely more detached experience when you are in a vehicle, as opposed to being on foot. The roads were a little flatter than we had been used to, and the buildings were slightly more substantial, but there was a familiarity about the main task, of making reconnaissance patrols across a landscape dominated by poppy fields.

The big picture revealed the undercurrents of the conflict. An influential tribal leader, Mullah Abdul Salaam, defected to the allies in the build-up to the operation, neutralizing around a third of the Taliban's fighting force. The coalition's strategic aim was to drive a wedge between so-called tier-two insurgents, less committed to the cause, and ideologically driven militants.

The Afghan army symbolically seized the town after three days without sustained resistance from the Taliban, who retreated in cold, foggy conditions. The local cottage industry was exposed by the discovery of a drug factory containing heroin worth up to £200 million on the open market. It was subsequently burned by British troops.

Insurgents tried, and failed, to draw us into the sort of response in which civilian casualties are incurred. It's a standard tactic, enacted in war since time immemorial. In this case it was clearly designed to compensate a military setback with a propaganda coup. Almost immediately, the Taliban increased the intensity of their attacks on British positions in Sangin.

At around this time military strategists were promoting the idea of forging alliances with ethnic tribesmen, a tactic that had worked, to a limited degree, in Iraq. We played a full role in a wider hearts-and-minds campaign designed to counter the impression of us as Western colonialists.

I genuinely believed in the value of practical development pro-grammes, which involved delivering food and medical supplies to villagers, who were offered weekly clinics and access to dental care. We handed out footballs and sweets to the kids, whose curiosity was insatiable. I'm not making a political point here, but ultimately aren't we all human beings? I tried to put myself in their place. As I admit-ted earlier, I would probably have taken up arms against a supposed invader, if the roles had been reversed. Can you imagine the anguish of a parent, who has never experienced peace, knowing their chil-dren are going to be trapped in the same cycle of violence?

Casualties are inevitable in war. One horrible image, of a father running towards Inkerman with a bloodied child in his arms, beg-ging for help, stays with me. We took him in, and our medics saved his child's life. Those moments of common humanity are deeply per-sonal, almost spiritual. They give you a sense of balance.

That was much-needed, since we were confronted by regular examples of man's inhumanity to man.

The Taliban took revenge on tribal leaders who accepted aid. In many cases they were summarily executed; some severed heads were left on spikes. We regularly came across bodies hanging in small copses of trees on the outskirts of a village. They were left there as a warning to the locals and to us, that we would suffer similarly if we were captured.

It is a terrible thing to contemplate, but such barbarism, and the terror it generates, overrides the morality of helping people. That is the reality of war. It's just the way it is. It's hard to reconcile the dynamics of the situation. Some locals did want to help us. They craved a quieter, better life. But they were too afraid to do anything about it.

Our tour of duty lasted 201 days. The shelling was incessant. We had forty-five significant contacts with insurgents; it took time and personal reflection to come to terms with each and every one. The mental strain is relentless; it is impossible to switch off. Under that sort of pressure it is no wonder some people crack.

One of our guys lost all sense of reason and had to be sent home for his own good, and for the company's peace of mind. Unprovoked, he started screaming and waving his rifle at a group of detainees, who had been brought in for questioning after having been seen behaving suspiciously. He was consumed with paranoia. When he took his aggression to another level and started menacing us with his weapon when we intervened, we realized he was on the verge of doing something stupid. He'd had enough. The safest and most urgent option was to get him out of there. It had all become too much.

We all left a little of ourselves at Inkerman. We built a memorial to Dee and other victims of the conflict, a mound of stones on which a wreath of poppies was laid beneath a large wooden cross, and gathered to pay our final respects. Inkerman, like most other FOBs, was eventually overrun, as the nature of the conflict changed. I simply can't bear to think of what has happened to that rough-and-ready but heartfelt monument.

It is as if he, and we, were never there.

SIX

Finding Myself

TRY SHAKING A can of lager for ten minutes, then opening it. It shouldn't come as any surprise when you, the floor, the ceiling and the walls are smothered in sweet, sticky stuff. In human terms, that's what happens when a company of Commandos is released from a daily cycle of danger, fear, violence, boredom and excitement, stretched over six months.

The Fun Bus, a C-17 bound for RAF Akrotiri on the southern tip of Cyprus, lifted off from Camp Bastion at 0632 on 15 April 2008. It carried a cargo of bootnecks ready to go on a three-day bender, known in the military as third-location decompression. What's not to like about water sports, gigantic barbecues and as much free booze as you can drink?

That may sound like the ultimate Club 18-30 holiday, but the psychological theory behind it was developed during the Vietnam War, when troops returning directly to the US from combat caused havoc because of their inability to reintegrate immediately into everyday life. Studies on combat motivation reach the fairly obvious conclusion that morale is dependent on membership of a tightly knit social group. It follows, then, that guys who have literally put their bodies on the line for one another wind down together. The combination of massive relief and instant relaxation needs some containing.

We were put up in a glorified holiday camp, with no outsiders permitted. Some bright spark decided to get the party started by shouting 'Naked bar!', an instruction that Marine tradition insists must be obeyed, whatever the circumstances. In no time at all a hundred or so blokes were stark bollock naked, chatting and laughing as if it was the most natural thing in the world.

Kit off, cocks out, get some drink down your neck.

If that was not sufficiently random, a mate of mine, Johnny Appleton, somehow got hold of a morphine pen from a medical kit. He was so drunk he was convinced that injecting himself was a great idea. Inevitably, he passed out and, after being checked over, was carried to his chalet, which looked, and smelled, like a cross between a garden shed and a latrine. Equally inevitably, he awoke the following day with the hangover from hell, and threw up constantly. He expected, and received, nothing but relentless piss-taking. He couldn't decide what was worse, the retching or the knowledge he was wasting another chance to drink his body weight in beer.

The contrast with the dutiful sons, brothers and husbands who disembarked at RAF Brize Norton seventy-two hours later was surreal. A homecoming is a huge event, celebrated by families and friends. Children wave home-made banners for their fathers, wives shed tears of joy at the safe return of their loved ones, and the car park is turned into a forest of flags. It's a great day, a real moment.

But for me, walking out into the crowds, it was just another day at the office. There was no one there to greet me. My mates piled into cars, to go home to family parties, and start the endless recycling of war stories. I was the only one who had to catch the camp orphan coach back to Taunton.

Norton Manor was deserted. It was pretty much me and the guard duty at the front gate, in splendid isolation. I just cracked on with it. It didn't bother me at the time as much as it does now, but at least I have made my peace with who I was and who I have become.

I buried the hurt deep down, and told myself I didn't need anyone to talk through what had been a life-changing experience. I was shut off, a little different. I didn't feel lonely. I felt I was living. I felt complete and fulfilled. This was what I was born to do, born to be. I had finally found my place.

I was out in the wide, wild world. I was becoming the man I wanted to be, someone shaped by experience, good and bad. I wasn't the sort to sit there crying in the corner. I didn't want to die quietly, feeling I had wasted my life. I wanted to slide into my grave, thinking, 'Fuck, that was awesome.'

Don't ask me why, but I guess, in some strange way, I instinctively knew the price of that attitude. I knew it would probably mess me up, on some level, but was willing to accept the consequences. My sadness today, coming to terms with a lost life, followed by a second chance at contentment, is almost a self-fulfilling prophecy.

The immediate sense of loss was harder to get to grips with. Since I had no visitors, I was happy to escort Dee Mulvihill's family and fiancée around the camp at the open day, a couple of weeks later. It was a lovely summer's day, with the smell of barbecues circulating on a warm wind, but tinged with understandable sadness.

I wanted them to know how popular the big man had been, how important he had been to me. I spoke about brotherhood, and the power of his example. I hoped they would find a degree of comfort in the tree planted in his honour at the camp. It was one of three, next to a memorial stone; the other two were a tribute to John Thornton and David Marsh, who were killed in a car bomb blast the month after Dee.

The seven hundred or so men from 40 Commando who gathered that afternoon represented a spiritual family rather than a biological one. We took real pride in the news that Lieutenant Colonel Stuart Birrell, our commanding officer, had just been awarded the Distinguished Service Order in recognition of 'gallant and distinguished services in Afghanistan'.

No one needed any reminding that his clear thinking, tactical nous and insightful leadership had saved many lives.

We received our campaign medals, with due pomp and ceremony, without forgetting the sacrifice of others. Hard men had moist eyes and cheered without embarrassment when Mark Ormrod, who had lost both legs and his right arm, and Ben McBean, who lost a leg and an arm, climbed out of their wheelchairs to walk 30 metres across the parade ground to receive their awards.

They're special people.

Mark, who had stepped on a landmine on Christmas Eve 2007, is one of those role models who find strength and inspiration in adversity. He has raised thousands for charity, competed in the Invictus Games for injured veterans, and acts as a motivational speaker and performance coach. That's what being the best of the best is all about.

The incentive to live for the day was irresistible. Before returning to sort out the rest of my life, I blew eight months' back pay, and a service bonus, on a riotous month or so in California with two mates from the troop, Mudders and Asbo, whose nickname offers a hint of what we got up to on our road trip from Los Angeles to Las Vegas, via San Francisco.

We tried to live like rock stars, staying in plush hotels, crashing at house parties, lurching around strip clubs and taking on the tables at a series of casinos. We also played the military card, going out in our Marine dress uniforms with some similarly dressed US Marines on Memorial Day. It was impossible for us to buy a drink.

We were in an adult playground, and bought tickets for what turned out to be a legendary UFC lightweight title fight between B. J. Penn and Sean Sherk at the MGM Grand. Penn won a brutal grudge match, and, in a signature move, licked the blood of his opponent off the back of his gloves. The place went nuts.

The rest of what went on in Vegas stays in Vegas, though I am prepared to admit my relationship with a waitress at Hooters was not based on the quality of the burgers she served. Asbo dived in a little deeper with a girl he met at a pool party. She was minted, and so besotted she flew him to northern California for a weekend together.

There was an end-of-era feel to our jolly boys' outing. We knew when we returned to the UK we would be split up in the various drafts from 40 Commando. We refer to it as being 'pinged' – essentially being recycled every two years to branches of the Corps that need replenishment. I was being nudged towards a role as a weapons specialist, but looked for loopholes in the system.

I asked to be classified as a swimmer/canoeist, and ended up working what we call 'behind the wire', guarding nuclear submarines at Faslane on the west coast of Scotland, some 25 miles from Glasgow. That might have mysterious, faintly thrilling connotations, but in reality it was mundane. I hated it, but never lost sight of the underlying reason why I pushed for the posting.

I had made my mind up to do all I could to join the Special Forces, preferably the Special Boat Service in Poole. Faslane fitted perfectly into the plan, since it incorporated long periods of downtime. The surrounding terrain, hilly and mountainous, was an ideal setting to train and hone my navigation and groundwork skills.

I was restless the moment I realized there was a level I could reach beyond the Marine Corps. I trust that doesn't imply disrespect, because they gave me values to live by, but the SF world just called out to me. Once I have made my mind up on anything I am incredibly stubborn. There wasn't a sliver of doubt in my mind that I would beat the odds.

It's not the sort of job you apply for on LinkedIn.

When the whispers began to circulate, that there was a phenomenal group of human beings I could join, I was hooked. People were in awe of these secretive, super elite soldiers. It was as if they were mystical, spectral presences who walked among us without us realizing.

It's hard to do your research, because elite units do not invite scrutiny. No one really knows what the job entails, so you go in blind. You hear half-cocked stories, torrents of bullshit from people who don't know what they're talking about. The attraction is still magnetic.

I've always gone one step beyond. The challenge chimed with my character.

I didn't always show it, but I was smart and self-reliant. The Special Forces do not operate on generic military principles. Instead of asking how high when ordered to jump by an officer, you are expected to work out the best method of doing so, and the optimal height that is achievable. Discipline is assumed, but a different mentality is demanded. Your character is mission critical.

Macho meatheads are weeded out by the selection process. The term you hear a lot during training is 'thinking man's soldier'. You are expected to think laterally, quickly, and decisively. It is not a job for someone who does exactly what they are told. There's no manual on how to deal with the unexpected or the unknown. There are no babysitters in a combat zone. You are expected to think for yourself, act on your own initiative. Precision is essential, because things must be done properly, but it isn't a straitjacket. Daring to be different when faced with life-or-death decisions takes moral courage rather than blind bravery. It requires mental strength rather than brute strength.

At that level, rank is almost a formality. The selection process flips convention on its head in looking for the individual who responds to the collective ethos. Officers get no preferential treatment; on the course they fulfil the same roles as raw candidates or non-commissioned ranks. You pass, or fail, as a team. The integrity of the unit is paramount.

This might not fit the mythology, but the culture of the SBS is holistic, and sets great store by the development of softer skills. It values academic achievement: time and credits are provided to pay for formal education, through online courses, up to degree level. To be promoted to a senior NCO you need to have minimum qualifications, such as a Maths A level.

In addition to speaking to Dee in Afghanistan, I had quietly picked the brains of a contingent from the Special Military Unit, who conducted some sneaky beaky operations from FOB Inkerman. One of them gave me the spur I needed. 'Give it a nudge and see what happens,' he advised. 'Put in for it. They can only say come back in four years . . .' So when a couple of SF guys gave an understated briefing on selection procedures during a post-op visit to Norton Manor, I began to put out feelers in earnest. The reaction was mixed: younger guys, on the whole, were more encouraging; older heads suggested I needed to wait, and serve my time. It was rare, almost unheard of, for such a young Marine to put himself forward. I was barely twenty-three.

The first hurdle was overcome when the commanding officer of my troop, Lieutenant Ed Middleton, gave his blessing. He had recently passed out from officer training, wasn't that much older than me, and identified with my ambition. My sergeant major, Andy Brownrigg, had his doubts, but testified to my military qualities, and the application drifted off into a twilight world of checks and balances.

In the meantime, I needed to make the most of Faslane, a place of marked contrasts. Security was understandably oppressive, given the presence of nuclear missiles and the Trident submarine fleet. It was a warren of massive hangars, which had the feel of Cold War intrigue and unwritten spy dramas. The waters are deep, easily navigable, and allow access to submarine patrol zones in the North Atlantic. The place has had nuclear associations since 1971, seven years after the modern base was established, but dates back to the First World War, and steam-powered submarines.

Entering the base involved running the gauntlet of peace protestors, who periodically attempted to handcuff themselves to the front gates. Their camp, established in 1982, seemed stuck in a time warp from the psychedelic sixties. In a strangely suburban touch, the main protest of the week was always held on a Wednesday.

With apologies to the local tourist board, the weather on the eastern shore of Gare Loch, to the north of the Firth of Clyde, is dreary. It's always pissing down. But the spirit is lifted by the natural beauty that surrounds the base. The loch is 10 kilometres in length, around 1.5 kilometres wide, and home to pods of porpoise and several species of seal. A bottlenose whale was even spotted there in 2020. The scenery is stunning, but my interest lay in its deceptive challenges and rewards.

While others went home on leave, within five minutes of walking out of the front gates I was heading straight for sweeping glens, steep hills and rugged mountain ranges, studded by huge boulders. It was another world, of beautiful nothingness. This was the province of ancient clans, like the MacAulays. It was a place of ghosts, and riddles posed by the ruins of medieval castles and chapels. I was on my own, having taken five days' boil-in-the-bag rations from the store at the base, and packed a poncho, bivi tent and gas cooker into my Bergen. I carried water, but knew I could drink from clear, cold streams.

I stopped off at the Marines HQ and badgered the weapons specialists for small-scale maps of the Highlands. With no speed-marching tracks available, I planned my own routes. I was confident in my fitness, since I had been running to Helensburgh and back – the equivalent of a half marathon – on a regular basis.

The sense of freedom, of being in the great outdoors, was sudden and uplifting. It was just me and nature, separate entities but part of an interconnected world. I had a great affinity with isolation; normality, for me, did not require company. I was comfortable with being alone. I preferred it, to tell the truth.

I felt dwarfed by nature, an insignificant speck on the landscape.

My senses surrendered to the hills and mountains, which stretched as far as the eye could see. No one knew where I was. I didn't have a safety beacon or emergency radio. If I had broken a leg, or wrecked an ankle, I would have been screwed. That was really stupid, but there was something spiritual about the experience that drew me in regardless.

These solo treks gave me a lot of time to think, almost on a different level. You leave all the bullshit, all the conventions we invent for ourselves, behind. It's so quiet it is as if you can actually hear your thoughts. When you acknowledge you are part of something bigger than yourself, you really get to know yourself.

What did I learn about myself?

It's a difficult question, perhaps the most difficult question to answer. It's hard to find the right words, in all honesty. The implications of getting under your own skin can be daunting. Finding out whether I was as tough as I wanted to be was pretty much the easy part.

My mind was open. Time seemed to slow down. When you commit to living in the moment, you let go completely. You see through the facade, the everyday delusion of people trying to be someone they are not. You feel no need for pretence. This is it. This is me. I learned that there can be release in risk.

I'd been hearing warnings about being careful what I wished for since childhood. I distinctly remember my mother telling me, 'One day you're going to push it too far, and you're going to get hurt.' I couldn't help it. I still feel the same way, despite everything. Tell me I can't do something and I'll do anything to prove you wrong.

I knew I had made a fundamental life decision in setting my sights on the SBS. I was fully aware that I had started on a journey from which there was no coming back. I realized, to my surprise, how much I loved life. I needed to know what I was capable of, what limits I could push myself towards. I find it strangely appealing that I've never discovered the extent of my boundaries.

The next moment of clarity I experienced during my time in Scotland was so disturbing it altered my outlook on life.

I was on a night out in Glasgow, chatting up a girl outside a club in Sauchiehall Street, when we were approached by a bloke who thought it was the height of wit to take the piss out of my accent. Original, eh? He wouldn't get off my case, and started to threaten me. When he threw a punch, I just snapped, and flew at him like a madman. I was in a blind rage, and had him in a headlock. I wanted to kill him. I didn't care who saw me do so, or what the consequences would be. My only conscious thought was that I had a choice between choking him and snapping his neck. I knew I had the opportunity and capability to do either. He couldn't breathe.

Thankfully, the red mist cleared, and sanity returned – just in time. I realized the enormity of the moment, understood the magnitude of the crime I was in danger of committing. I let him go, and picked him up, weeping and apologizing for what I had done. He started lashing out and tried to headbutt me, but, still crying, I kept him pinned against the wall until he calmed down.

I'd never known such anger. Looked at logically, it was possibly a momentary episode of PTSD, but it felt like an exorcism. Everything poured out of me. All the hidden demons, dragged into the light during that manifestation of madness, were put to flight.

We all have our breaking points, and I had found mine. I recognized, in that instant, that my training and experiences had changed me fundamentally. I could never again complacently consider myself a normal member of society, because of my potential to inflict harm. I could never go around doing what I wanted, because I had the capacity to kill.

With great power comes great responsibility.

That sort of self-awareness and self-discipline is integral to the SF soldier. He cannot be a whack job, unable to control his actions or emotions. He must respect his strength, and never succumb to his ego. Looking back now, that was the moment that taught me the type of character I needed to be, to live up to my expectations.

To this day, I don't know why the unit accepted my application to attend the five-day briefing course which decided whether I deserved the privilege of being allowed to be among the select few drawn annually from across the armed services, considered worthy candidates for selection trials. I'm committing a cardinal sin here, since the service does not indulge guesswork, but I imagine they had their own intelligence sources, and someone played a hunch.

Elite units are in a perpetual cycle of evolution and renewal, as befits their elite status, so I wasn't surprised to learn that the briefing course I attended has been superseded, in an era of greater integration. It is now a joint exercise, but the demands are as taxing as ever. That's as it should be – as it must be.

I was instructed to report to Poole in October 2008, barely six months after returning from Afghanistan. In addition to my running and trekking, I had been busting my guts in the gym at Faslane, where I still had to fulfil the rest of my duties and cram in extra sentry sessions to compensate for my impending absence. If I wanted to aim at the stars there would be no free ride.

My feelings, on the plane to Bournemouth, mirrored those I had struggled to contain on my original train journey from Bristol to the Marines training centre at Lympstone. There was an identical sense of dread, that I had pushed myself in over my head. One inner voice was reassuring ('You've come so far, you can't back out now') while the other – 'Shit, shit, shit! I'm going to get found out so badly they'll mug me off in no time' – was on the edge of hysteria.

I was by far the youngest and least experienced of around thirty guys being put through their paces. The group was relatively small, but it quickly became clear it contained special people. I felt an immediate affinity with a man who, for me, embodies the qualities of the elite operative.

Nirmal Purja is known by his nickname, 'Nims'. He is a Nepalese climber who excelled in the Gurkhas before serving in the SBS. In 2019 he scaled the world's fourteen highest mountains in a record time of six months and six days, taking only forty-eight hours to reach the death zone summits of Everest, Lhotse and Makalu. His legendary status was confirmed in January 2021, when he completed the first winter ascent of K2. A tattoo of those fourteen mountains, inscribed across his back, reveals the spirituality which accompanies quiet strength. The ink was blended with DNA from the hair of his parents, brothers, sister and wife.

He was only two years older than me – another relative rookie in the group – but his bearing, persistence, intelligence and humility left an indelible impression.

The human chemistry of an elite soldier still fascinates me. Some essential virtues – control, courage and clarity of thought – are pretty easy to detect. The difference is the X factor, an intangible asset that has as much to do with personality as military excellence, which is regarded as a given. It's a people business, when all is said and done.

The briefing course was my first opportunity to meet serving SF soldiers in their own domain. Their presence might have been casual, but there was nothing accidental about their message. They respected my rawness and reassured me that I would be judged no differently from the others because of my youth. That lifted my morale, because they spoke to me as an equal.

A more traditional pecking order was rapidly imposed in the candidates' accommodation block. Experienced sergeants gravitated together, and took control. I looked up to the mountain leaders, drawn from the Marines. They were arctic warfare instructors, cold weather survival specialists, experts in climbing and cliff assault techniques. I was seen as the sprog, the kid. That was fine by me, since I doubted anyone would have worked harder to be there. I was more concerned by degrees of difficulty.

The Marines pre-selection course at Lympstone might have been tough, but compared to this examination it was a stroll to a country pub, as opposed to an unaided trek to the South Pole. They basically thrashed us, from first light and through the night. We did brutal fitness tests, timed speed marches, and navigation exercises in darkness. They took weapon training to another level, and once sleep deprivation began to bite threw in tactical challenges and complicated map-reading sessions for good measure. Everything, from combat skills to character traits under pressure, was scrutinized, analysed, logged. There was an element of psychological probing, but it was relatively mild. They were looking for confidence, and on the alert for arrogance. I can't lie, though. When a few of the sergeants began to fall by the wayside, it gave me a lift.

I know this sounds terrible, but I knew I was very good at my job. My mates in the Corps called me Pusser, Royal Navy slang for the ship's purser. Since he was responsible for the daily rum rations and the distribution of basic equipment, he had to be efficient or risk inciting a mutiny. I was known for carefully dotting my i's and crossing my t's. I aspired to do everything by the book, as I was taught, but wasn't afraid to go off script if necessary. I took care with the basics, weapons drills and everyday disciplines, and took pride in my efficiency. That didn't come without hard work, and constant practice. I was very strict with myself: I pushed myself to meet expectations, because I would not have forgiven failure.

If the directing staff and the training team saw anything in me, they kept it close to their chests. Any praise is kept in-house, as a state secret. The trainers were something else. They'd been there, done the big jobs, and had no need to boast. They knew the importance of the bloodline.

Fewer than ten of us would make it to the next stage. The post-course briefing left doors open without indicating whether I would be allowed to re-enter later that winter. I had to return to Scotland, wait, and wonder.

SEVEN

Endure

IT'S MIDNIGHT. A blizzard is raging across the Brecon Beacons. I've just done a 42-kilometre march, in waist-deep snow, and I'm being immediately sent back out to do the equivalent of another marathon. Even when a milky version of dawn begins to break, it is impossible to see more than 5 feet in front of my face.

Some guys are so tired they forget to keep eating, a terrible mistake when you are burning at least 6,000 calories a day in sub-zero temperatures. They're done for, and will be withdrawn soon. The SBS selection course is not a vindictive process, but an assessment of your ability to respond to extreme physical and psychological challenges.

Weaknesses will emerge. There's no shame in failure, although regret will linger and, in some cases, sour. By the end of the initial five-week endurance phase, less than 20 per cent of the candidates will remain.

I'm marching on adrenaline, mini pork pies and slices of a Mighty Meat pizza, topped with pepperoni, ground beef, ham, sausage, mushrooms and red onions, ordered on the sly from Domino's, and pre-packed in a Tupperware container. In addition to food and water, I'm carrying an 80lb pack and my rifle. I am also necking bottles of concentrated protein shake, given to me by a mate on the course, who had acquired them from his father, a cancer patient. You learn to be resourceful in seeking any advantage or assistance: that pizza trick was passed on by one of the old boys I made a point of chatting to during the pre-selection exercises in Poole.

I was very aware of my inexperience and wasn't afraid to ask for tips from guys who had been there, and done it. They were more than willing to help, because they knew the value of continual learning, and probably identified with my eagerness. I never hid the fact I wanted to be like them.

Basic disciplines get you through those back-to-back marathons, which must be completed in eighteen hours. In the brief break before you return to the Beacons, which have a military history dating back to cavalry bases in Roman times, you dry your kit, especially your boots and socks, as best you can. You talc your feet, dress your blisters, ignore the temptation to shut your eyes.

Lads have been consistently falling by the wayside since the Fan Dance at the end of the first week. It's a notorious four-hour test march over Pen y Fan, at nearly 3,000 feet the highest mountain in the Brecon range. You climb the western slope, descend on the other side, and retrace your route back to the summit via Jacob's Ladder, a wickedly steep path along which you scramble on hands and knees, before returning to the original checkpoint.

The Beacons are forbidding, even without a whiteout. Abandoned training camps, firing ranges and the rusted wreckage of crashed aircraft are being slowly repossessed by nature. The weather system is unusual because the Beacons is the first land mass hit by the jet stream. Cloud drops suddenly, sending temperatures plummeting, and impairing visibility.

In such an uncontrollable environment, people get lost and dehydrated. Hypothermia sets in, with fatal consequences. Each death in training or selection is a tragedy that requires the exhaustive scrutiny of an official inquiry, but we know the score. Bad things can happen.

We have the insurance of a beacon inside our backpacks, which reveals geographical location and acts as a deterrent against the desperation that can lead to the unthinkable – an attempt to cheat. Each march is an exercise in self-regulation. You must think your way around, tread carefully while moving quickly across the rocky landscape, and pick the right tracks to follow.

Did I ever get close to giving up because of the perpetual punishment?

Every. Single. Day.

You're up at 4 a.m., even when you are allowed the luxury of sleep. You're exhausted, permanently hungry. Your back aches. Your feet are shredded and sore, since you are on them all day, applying pressure as you trudge through snow, slush, swamps and bogs. You suffer from pins and needles in your toes, and you sweat despite being freezing. No wonder you question your sanity.

Do you have the ability to push, and keep on pushing, yourself when every fibre of your body is telling you to call it a day? Are you willing to go the distance? The process is designed to answer the question you dare not speak aloud: what is my breaking point?

I never found mine until that bullet paralysed me.

I coped with selection, and the hardships of the SF world, but getting up every day, and keeping going, as a quadriplegic is by far the hardest thing I have ever done. I do it, but don't really know why I do it. I'm not afraid to say that I've occasionally reached the point where I wanted to end my life because I find it just too hard.

I was trained by the SBS to endure, but ops had a point of completion. Tours of duty had a defined length. I have had to accept there is no end to this. The pain will never go away. The suffering, the longing to be part of normal life, will never leave me. When you have nothing to hold on to you have to find a purpose.

In a way, I know I'm fucked. I've come to terms with that. But I tell myself I still have a warrior's spirit. I look at it as the glass being half full; I've still got a lot to live for. I'm determined not to be dependent on one person, a particular drug, or the false hope of a miracle cure, promoted by con men. My problem is finding fulfilment. How do I go on from here?

To answer that question means reuniting, mentally at least, with that young lad who coped with everything the SBS course directors could throw at him. 'Marine, heal thyself' doesn't quite have the ring of the old line about the physician, but the same principle applies. I'm searching for that kid to give me a reason to believe.

My purpose in outlining some of the tests I passed is not to sustain the myth that I was some sort of superman. I respect the delicacy of some of the details, and would never do anything to impinge on current operational procedures, but the perspective of what I went through is important if you wish to understand me, then and now.

The psychological trials are intense, and peel away the layers of your personality. They purposely blur boundaries, and force you to address primal fears. Observers need to know how you react to being isolated or compromised. They test your powers of concentration and determination, since a momentary lack of attention to detail on an operation can be deadly.

There's nothing remotely superficial in playing the role of fugitive. It becomes frighteningly real the moment you are dropped in the middle of nowhere with nothing but a compass, a 1:25 map and a solitary twenty-four-hour ration pack, which has to last a week. You must travel between checkpoints, avoiding capture while being hunted down by dogs, helicopters and hostile groups in a range of vehicles.

You don't have a clue where you are. It could be anywhere, though in my case, by studying the terrain, I reckoned I was in Scotland. Ultimately, though, my location was irrelevant. If I was captured I could kiss my chances of selection goodbye. That was an existential threat I didn't want to contemplate. I quickly became feral, sensing danger sometimes where it did not exist.

There was no point in travelling by day, since detection was almost certain. I had to hide until darkness fell, and navigate by the stars. Nervous, surreptitious progress meant I could cover only about 18 miles a night. I drank from mountain streams, lived off the land as best I could, and slept, protected from the elements, in hay bales or deserted outbuildings.

The sense of jeopardy is haunting. Even though you know the evasion phase is a simulation, you are genuinely scared. You are being pursued by other army regiments, who find it a pretty cool job to do. You're told beforehand that if you are caught your captors will not fuck about. You're going to get a beating.

I know what you're thinking – what, by your own guys?

That's just how it is. In a way, it is a measure of the professionalism of the process. Think about it: out in the field there will be no second chances. The potential brutality of your preparation could save your life. The test is meant to seize your imagination and demand your full attention, so it cannot feel inauthentic. You have to be hyper-aware of your vulnerability. For that to happen it must feel like the real deal.

The course directors know roughly where you are, and want to discover how far you will push yourself. Strategically, you are kept on edge, and presented with a series of choices that reveal important aspects of your character. It is common, for instance, to find a large, fast-flowing river between you and your destination. Again, it looms up in the middle of the night.

The cold is eating into your bones. Are you going to take the risk of the easy route, like a bridge or a simple crossing point? Or are you going to give yourself the best chance of survival by doing the hard yards, wading across waist-deep water in the darkness in the knowledge your trousers and boots won't dry for at least forty-eight hours? There aren't too many launderettes in the wilderness.

How disciplined are you? How mentally strong will you be under strain?

It is easy for me to say now, but I loved it. I drew on my survival training, which began in the Marines, where you are taught how to set snares, how to kill a rabbit humanely, skin it, and recognize which internal organs can be eaten. I successfully evaded my pursuers, reached the final checkpoint, and was plunged into a whole new world of pain.

The next phase of selection, designed to test your capability to operate under duress, begins immediately, with a recreation of capture.

Logically you know what is coming, since the resistance element of selection has its own mythology among the candidates, but you are shattered physically, and shaken mentally. It all feels as real as it could possibly be when you are ambushed.

It remains one of the most testing things I have ever done.

Your shoelaces are taken away, and you are placed into a stress position. This can range from kneeling for hours on hard, rutted floors to being prodded into standing awkwardly, so that muscles tense and seize. It can involve being subjected to white noise or sudden explosions of sound, which burrow into the brain.

The only time your blindfold is removed is when you are interrogated, bombarded with threats and leading questions designed to test whether you are still mentally in control of what you are saying. Can you keep your wits about you at the extremes of provocation? Do you have the selflessness to protect your mates at all costs?

Your captors usually push you into a bare room, with a concrete floor and a chair. Occasionally the setting has a darker, more sinister feel. The room is icy, wet, musty, threatening. Wherever you end up, you will be disorientated, because you will have been dragged around the interrogation complex precisely in order to scramble your senses. I didn't know if I was up or down, left or right, inside or outside. I'd been walked around in circles for what felt like hours. My brain was trying to process fleeting impressions of doorways and archways, sensed through the blindfold. I was hustled upstairs and pulled down again, several stairs at a time. Sometimes I felt wood beneath my feet. On other occasions I stumbled through gravel, or across rocks.

The mind games were incessant. My abductors pretended to whisper in my ear. They tapped me faintly on the shoulder. Every action was designed to generate fear, self-doubt and confusion. Lack of sleep meant I was on the cusp of reality and fantasy. I forced myself to focus by concentrating on a desperate inner conversation.

Tell them nothing, Tobes. Nothing.

The information they are trying to elicit is simple, but damning. They want you to admit you are a Western soldier. They laugh at your ineptitude, in being caught wearing a uniform. You try to bull-shit your way through it – I argued I had been given my kit as a game ranger – knowing that if it sounds too silly, you will get a beating.

Let's just say the interrogation techniques are far more intense than anything you might have seen on television programmes designed to recreate the SF experience. I know that sounds shock-ing, but remember the context. The object of the exercise is to see how much you can endure until they break you. They are trying to discover the limits of your self-control. When they're threatening to kill you or, worse, your fellow prisoners, your state of mind is so warped you do not doubt their intent.

It requires powers of resistance you never knew you possessed. It is only when you recognize a pre-briefed signal that you know it is over. You're not told you have passed, but I was buzzing, absolutely buzzing.

I completely lost track of time to the point I didn't know if it was night or day. It gave me confidence that I could remain in control under insidious pressure. Maybe I did have what it takes. Perhaps I could cope, through an acute form of self-discipline that enabled me to zone out when I was in peril.

A handful of us remained at the end of the phase; some good men simply cracked under the constant stress, and voluntarily withdrew. I benefited from the experience because it taught me about the man I could become. That, deep down, was the driving force behind my determination to become an elite soldier. I wanted to test myself. I wanted to see if I could do something beyond 99.99 per cent of the population.

The jungle phase of selection in South East Asia, where we were flown immediately after the initial endurance tests, was the other pinch point in the weeding-out process. It represents a fundamental test of military capability. Your discipline must be phenomenal, because the environment is so alien. The place literally eats you alive.

There are so many things to deal with. Ticks drink your blood. You are stalked by local forces, which play the role of the enemy. Heat and humidity drain the body and soften the mind. Water must be purified if you are to avoid dysentery. Trench foot is a recurring problem, if your feet are not kept dry and clean. You wrap your shit in clingfilm and store it in your backpack, because you must not leave a scent.

The mud is caramel-coloured sludge that sucks you in. You must be aware of every single movement, since each carries the danger of telegraphing your position. Failure to keep your rifle clean results in immediate exclusion, as does the cardinal sin of resting, even momentarily, against a tree trunk. Do that and you might as well sing a song to unseen trackers.

It is so easy to get lost, even when you painstakingly plant your feet in the indentations left by the previous guy. The jungle is so dense it is only possible to patrol short distances. It can take eight hours to carefully navigate 400 metres of barely penetrable vegetation. The canopy blots out all but slivers of sunlight. It is impossible to travel at night because you cannot see a thing.

I never took anything for granted, but by this stage I knew my resilience was repeatable, in almost all circumstances. The one remaining shard of doubt was triggered by the jumps phase of selection, which followed some basic examinations in signalling and radio work. It begins with the traditional Second World War leap from 1,000 feet, in which the draw cord of the parachute is pulled the instant you fall from the aircraft.

I tried hard to hide the awful truth, that I was terrified of heights. It hardly helped when the main chutes of a couple of mates failed to open in subsequent tests. You are taught to try and resolve the problem; if that is not possible you must cut it away. That means having the presence of mind to pull your reserve chute.

What happens if that also fails? Welcome to my recurring nightmare, from which I woke in panic in the middle of too many nights . . .

There was no way I was going to submit to my subconscious with the goal so close. I operated on automatic pilot through the rest of the disciplines, forming squares on descent, jumping off the back of a Hercules or a helicopter. My final aerial treats were reserved for pre-deployment training. HALO – free-falling from high altitudes, and opening the chute late, to avoid radar detection – was a daunting test of nerve that required complete self-control when my brain wanted to shut down.

I was better suited to surveillance exercises and the boats phase, but never lost sight of the fact I was being judged on my ability to adapt and learn on the job. Subsequent courses, which ranged from medical procedures to demolition, stretched me in different ways.

Why did only so few of us make it through selection? I have never looked at it from the other side, by taking potential recruits through the course, so can only offer my own perspective.

Just as there is no job description, there's no standard CV, or a set of boxes to be ticked. There are so many layers to each candidate that selection decisions are made on a personal basis. They dig into your background, examine you from all angles. Choices are underpinned by the knowledge that people are shaped by different circumstances, and have different attributes.

What becomes clear, if I look at the guys who have come through the system, is that the course directors are seeking complementary personal and professional qualities. Elite soldiers are very driven, extremely passionate. They have a fierce sense of personal identity. They are fantastically fit, habitually disciplined, and work smartly given freedom of choice to go the way they think best, without losing the cohesion of the unit.

Crucially, they have a strong moral backbone, a keen sense of right and wrong, based on individually held principles rather than a standard rule book. There's an acceptance that they are always under scrutiny and, very occasionally, the facade drops. The emergence of deeply hidden character defects, such as unchecked arrogance or aggression, usually results in the individual being returned to his unit. An RTU leaves an indelible stain.

People don't do this job because they want to be a celebrity, or to act as Billy Big Wig in the local nightclub. They're phenomenal people, but you'd never realize that if you saw them in the pub, on the street, or in Tesco. You wouldn't give them a second glance. They don't stand out. They neither want nor need credit for their achievements. They dislike praise. Accepting it is almost seen as a sign of weakness.

To tell the truth, I'm a bit of a control freak. I don't like being told I cannot do something. That really gets my back up. Something inside says, 'Oh, really?' I don't know if that is blind arrogance or sheer stupidity, but I react as if the world is daring me to prove it wrong.

I hate being told I should be proud of what I've done. It gets on my nerves. I suppose, on some deeper psychological level, that is a defence mechanism. If I accepted I was special – which I don't – I'd lose my edge. I've got a need, even now, to keep pushing myself. Nothing is ever good enough. I'm almost an over-perfectionist.

The inner conversation goes something like this: 'I am not good enough. I need to study. I need to practise. I need to get better because he is better than me. Why am I not as good as him? I've got to keep striving. Otherwise, what's the point?'

Competitiveness is balanced by the central truth of being a Special Forces soldier. Whatever you do, it is about the group rather than the individual. Accolades are unnecessary because only we know what it takes. We are only as good as the people around us. We don't go around patting each other on the butt and saying, 'Good job, mate.' Respect is mutual and unspoken. I really miss that.

Again, to be brutally honest, I had reservations about doing this book. I didn't want this to be seen as some sort of attempt to project myself as the big 'I am'. I knew what I was signing up for, so have no complaints about what happened to me. I'm just trying to find something positive in a shitty situation, and help a few people, in similar positions to me, along the way.

It took a long, long time for me to decide to share my story. I wouldn't have done so without the support of my former comrades. They tell me I can inspire others. Those friendships, forged in battle, mean more to me than anything. It's a special feeling.

I have never forgotten the surge of pride I felt upon being accepted into the regiment. Though I was desperate to share the news, I respected the code of secrecy and told no one. In fact the first time my mum and stepdad knew what I did for a living was when a senior official from the South African government, a high-ranking military man, appeared on their doorstep to tell them I had been hurt in action, and was on the verge of death.

There's a quiet, deeply affecting dignity about the formal process of being welcomed in the officers' mess in Poole. The commanding officer gives a short speech, makes a champagne toast, and then presents you with a beret (with SBS cap badge) and a belt (with SBS logo on the clasp). The belt is green; the SAS belts are blue.

Those berets tend only to be worn on camp, or during official ceremonies. When military people see the insignia, they give you instinctive respect. They look at you a little differently. Not because they're in awe of you, but because they know you are very, very good at your job. Any aura is not created by you but by the successes and sacrifices of previous generations.

Once the formalities are completed, the lads in the squadron gather on the helicopter landing pad on camp. Each newcomer must stand up in front of the group and give a two-minute speech about himself. It is a strange feeling, since you are beside yourself with happiness, but wary of going over the top. I managed to gabble something along the lines of 'I'm South African, a bit of a surfer dude. Before I got into the military I didn't really know what I was doing with my life. I decided to be the best man I can be and hope I will never let any of you down. It is an honour and a privilege to be accepted into the unit.'

I felt as if I had reached the centre of my universe. The feeling was so intense it was almost beyond camaraderie. It's uniquely emotional because you are joining a unique group of people.

Before we went out, for countless beers and a curry in town, there was one final ritual to complete, to honour the memory of a fallen comrade known to all in perpetuity by his nickname, Tosh. That involved downing two pints of Guinness and a tumbler of whisky in one go, from a flower vase shaped like a frog, while on one knee. The liquid, consumed through a hole in the frog's arse, floods out fast. Other squadrons have equally distinctive drinking vessels; one, for instance, uses a 105mm howitzer shell.

I'd done a yard of ale in a few pubs, so knew the basics of controlling my throat muscles to avoid taking a bath in the stuff as the rest of the guys counted how long it was taking. Once I'd finished, I obeyed tradition by raising the vase above my head before turning it upside down, to prove I'd drained the lot.

'Drinking In' means you have joined the grown-ups. When I reported to the regimental sergeant major for roll call at the start of my first official day, he looked as if I'd parachuted in from Pluto. 'What are you doing here?' he exclaimed. 'You're an adult now.' I was trusted to do my job.

We are known as the tip of the sword. We cut deep, draw blood, and make our enemies suffer.

EIGHT

Firebreak

THE FEATURES OF the first man I consciously killed have faded over time, but he never leaves me. The guilt I feel in having taken the life of a fellow human being is overwhelming, and often returns when I least expect it. The emotions involved are intense, almost indescribable, but I have no option but to live with the consequences of my actions.

It happened on a dark night during an early mission in the hinterland of Afghanistan, and involved what we call CQC, close quarter combat. This is essentially different from my experiences on patrol on my first tour with the Marines, where contact with insurgents tended to be conducted at long distance. I might well have been responsible for someone's death then, but there was a sense of detachment, because it was never corroborated.

This is not something I really want to talk about, but it needs to be confronted because it represents the reality of a soldier's existence. We take casualties and inflict casualties. We are both prey and predators. It is a dehumanizing process, because it is so unnatural.

Anyone who tells you it does not leave a scar is either a liar or a psychopath.

Everything happens so quickly in such circumstances, but death is, to some extent, anticipated. It literally comes with the territory. At some level, psychologically, you prepare for its probability by detaching yourself from the awful truth that you will be firing at someone's son, husband or father. It's simply kill, or be killed.

There have been other operations that I cannot go into in detail. You have a job to do, a mission to complete, but you are not a robot. However hard you try not to think about what you have done, it is impossible to ignore when you are unscrambling your senses on the helicopter back to base, or when you are finally alone, in the single room that is the privilege of the elite soldier.

We are all human. A fatal firefight takes its toll, messes with your head. It returns in a series of flashbacks, and toys with your imagination. It's unnatural. Your mind takes you to places you never knew existed and your sleep is shallow and disturbed. Grief, remorse and relief force you to contemplate what life is all about. I understand the morbid fascination with war. I accept and expect questions about its morality.

How can you live with yourself? You just do. What else can I say?

There are so many layers to the subject. The insurgent who paralysed me did so with a variant of the AK-47, the assault rifle invented by Mikhail Kalashnikov, an engineer and former Red Army lieutenant general, in 1947. It is estimated that a hundred million of them have been produced; Russian president Vladimir Putin hailed it as 'a symbol of the creative genius of our people'.

It is the deadliest weapon of the twentieth century, having been responsible for several million deaths in conflicts across the globe. To give a sobering comparison, the atom bombs dropped on Hiroshima and Nagasaki in August 1945 killed two hundred thousand.

Kalashnikov died a national hero, aged ninety-four, in 2013, having been awarded the Stalin Prize, the Red Star and the Order of Lenin. He persistently refused to acknowledge any sense of personal responsibility for so much suffering, telling one reporter, 'I sleep soundly.' However, just before his death he wrote to the head of the Russian Orthodox Church: 'The pain in my soul is unbearable. I keep asking myself the same unsolvable question. If my assault rifle took people's lives it means that I am responsible for their deaths.'

There is a horrible world out there. It is basic and cruel. We put ourselves in harm's way on SF operations because we are the hunters. This isn't your basic patrol, a calculated show of force to intimidate or discourage the enemy. We are deliberately picking a fight, and they invariably know we are coming. That means our mortality rate is higher than it would be in more conventional units.

It is yin and yang. We inflict more casualties on the other side. It's scary, pretty intense, and understandably takes its toll on your mind and body, since unchecked adrenaline and constant anxiety is a dangerous cocktail. You have no choice but to park your fears, both for yourself and your comrades, and concentrate on the task in hand.

It takes a certain type of person, possessing innate aggression and certainty of purpose, to go beyond logical limits. To enable me to put myself in harm's way, I would ask myself: Who are you? What are you made of? And I would tell myself never to give up. *Never surrender. This is not your time.* This mantra kept me going during the blackest, bleakest moments.

An elite soldier exists on the extremities of life. That involves fighting fire with fire, just as a bush fire can be controlled by the incineration of any vegetation in its path. Specialist units form a human firebreak, because they are prepared to match the calculated ruthlessness of their foes.

Maybe you need people like us in the free world. Faced with a pitiless enemy, you have to match their discipline and determination to go to any lengths to prevail. Sometimes the only way to defeat evil – and I use that word deliberately, from personal experience of Taliban brutality – is to make any sacrifice, do whatever it takes.

The leap of faith can be pretty bloody terrifying, because it begs huge questions and triggers deeply suppressed doubts. Can anyone be certain of anything in war? Are we fighting for a just cause? Why do the enemy believe their motives are as pure as ours? Are we simply a mirror image of each other? Are they experiencing the same emotions as they line us up in their sights? Who is to say they are wrong and I am right? Do they believe, like us, they are killing to save lives?

Thoughts like these are hard to wrap your head around. People deal with them in different ways, some better than others. I've seen many guys struggle. Friends break down piece by piece, drink by drink, drug hit by drug hit. Some lash out at society, and end up in trouble. It's terrible to watch.

I got through it by focusing on the bigger picture. Our principal role in Afghanistan was to pursue, capture and process the Taliban commanders and strategists. Our aim was to protect our troops on the ground from deadly ambushes, IEDs, and suicide bombers who represented a real and present threat.

How many lives can you save in the process of taking one life? How many bootnecks on the ground have you protected by taking out a big player? How many civilians have been spared needless tragedy? The numbers may be indistinct, but we had been briefed extensively on the history and characteristics of the men we pursued, with deadly intent.

It's not a blind search for vengeance. Intelligence reports showed that these targets were bad people. They had innocent blood on their hands. There were a lot of moving parts in the political, diplomatic and military spheres that needed to align if they were to be held accountable. Those decisions were made way above my pay grade. Most of my time was spent kicking doors in.

A lot of background work went into operations. The nature of the finds, from the quality of components to the nationality of any captives, offered important clues about the scope of enemy operations.

We were trying to cut the head off the snake. The Taliban operated on similar lines to an organized crime family or a drug cartel. Just as, elsewhere in the world, street hustlers and dealers operated as human shields for suppliers, foot soldiers were expendable. A culture of criminality was deeply embedded, and sustained by corrupt officials.

I'm sure you've all seen the FBI movies where photographs of gang members are clustered beneath portraits of the Godfather and his consigliere on a chalkboard. We had that sort of family tree back at base. Trust me, Kandahar Confidential was a lot more real than Hollywood fiction.

We would follow feeds from MQ-1 Predators, jet-powered unmanned aircraft developed by the US Air Force and the CIA. I liaised in real time with drone operators at the Indian Springs complex to the north of Las Vegas, advising them to focus on specific locations or groups of individuals. The cameras on the drones operated over huge distances; pictures were heat-sensitive and occasionally inverted, so that they offered a white image on a black screen for better clarity. Yet, in today's terms, we were in the Stone Age. The MQ-1 was taken out of service in 2018, twenty-three years after it was first used operationally, and replaced by the bigger, more sophisticated MQ-9 Reaper.

It's natural to concentrate on the machinery, but the quality of the men around you matters more.

You don't have to be under fire to get to know your unit, but bonds form really quickly. There's mutual respect, because you all know what you have been through to get there, but an unwritten pecking order, based on experience rather than formal rank, is established. You've got to prove yourself worthy of trust.

My first specialist operation was what we call a dry hole. There was no dramatic contact. We didn't find who we were looking for in the target compound. I wasn't to know that when we hit the ground, of course. I was really nervous, and, in trying to be as professional as possible by volunteering for everything, over-compensated for being the young pup. I wanted to show I deserved to be there. I was trying to imitate the body language of the guys around me. I saw a calmness and collectiveness in them that I desperately wanted to match. I tried my best, but wasn't fooling anyone. Everyone knew it was my first sharp-end experience. They weren't going to mollycoddle me, but they kept a watchful eye out. I looked up to them, and they quietly looked after me. There were no grand gestures, because that is not how things are done, but on early missions one of the guys might beckon me to sit next to him after we ran on to the helo. I'd be trying to be all macho, and he would see me for what I was – a rabbit in the headlights.

My inexperience didn't matter because I wanted to learn. I guess that's a sign of a good soldier. I pummelled the guys with questions: What techniques did they use? Why did they act in a certain way? Where's the best place to pack a pistol, your hip or chestplate? What about your rounds and your drop bag for empty magazines? What are the danger signs? They didn't need to say 'Don't worry, Tobes, you'll be fine' because they knew the eternal truth.

You adapt, or die.

You learn the hard way, or any way, but you have to learn pretty damn quick. There's no dummy run. When you're there, you're in it. Everything goes at a million miles an hour in your first assault. Despite the sound and fury, you can hear your heart racing in your chest – *bub bub*, *bub bub*, *bub bub*. You're asking yourself, 'What the fuck is going on? Where am I going? What am I doing?'

It takes a few operations to get a grip. I learned how to control my nervous energy. Instead of racing off the back of the helo on the landing zone like a headless chicken, I'd go into all-round defence, dropping on one knee and adjusting my night vision goggles before marching off in my stack, my order, towards the target.

If you don't stop twitching at every sound or unexpected sight you are going to burn yourself out, and become a liability. You learn what to look for, how to recognize a threat. Instead of being stressed, or shattered, you are sharp. You become battle-hardened, a phrase you once used about others with a sense of awe.

I learned how to be a proper SF soldier from the people around me. They were so in tune with one another. They taught me how to be proficient. No fuss, but so professional, clinical and in control. They knew how to come down from a horrible night in the field, how to hide the hurt with wicked humour. The worst thing you can do is cut yourself off, and become isolated.

The banter was brutal, tasteless to the point of being warped, but hilarious. We had door wars back at base, in which all sorts of shit would be plastered across the entrance to your room. As a South African, it was assumed I was a full-on racist. I had Ku Klux Klan signs and Nazi slogans daubed on my door, together with the obligatory photographs of Hitler and naked black chicks. No one knew who was posting the stuff, which usually appeared when you were out. I got off lightly compared to one of the guys who, in an inexplicable moment of weakness, admitted to having slept with a transvestite in Thailand. I'll leave the images he was confronted with to your imagination, but they were not for the faint-hearted.

A sense of belonging is subtle, silent. I felt connected, and the respect of my mates was unspoken. They had the confidence to allow me to be a point man, the guy who led the way into compounds and set the tempo of an attack. We knew the stakes: a couple of days before we arrived in theatre a unit had walked into an IED daisy chain while under fire.

The carnage devastated seasoned soldiers, who became sullen and reflective, and couldn't wait to get home. We quickly understood the heaviness of their mood. Our work was secretive, perilous, and unrelenting. We were in a daily cycle of restless sleep, continual briefing and nightly combat over a wide range. We regularly returned to base in the early hours.

Inevitably, we became blood brothers.

I was shot during what had seemed a routine job. We came in on helicopters; one hovered just above the ground in front of the suspect vehicles after delivering a warning shot for them to stop. This creates what we call a brown-out, a choking cloud of dust through which it is impossible to see. If the targets do not comply, and this leads to a so-called bomb burst, in which they scatter by driving in random directions, it obviously means they are as guilty as sin. That's usually not a problem, since the Predator tracks them. They can be mopped up later, once business is taken care of.

On this occasion, though, it all began to go wrong when they kept their nerve, probably out of sheer desperation. They sped off and disappeared into a nearby compound. We were about to discover how unlucky we had been.

We had no knowledge of the building into which they fled. We had no idea of how many insurgents we would find, or what type of weapons they held. For all we knew, the whole area could have been booby-trapped. Since nothing could be ruled out when it came to guerrilla activity, they might even have got wind of our intentions and were trying to sucker us into an ambush.

The situation called for an instant decision. We were not at full strength and, in the absence of our commanding officer, the regimental sergeant major had the responsibility of weighing up the value of the mission. I was with him in another helicopter. He made the call that we would have to go in blind, with the other helicopters providing an over-watch.

He didn't need to tell us that any hesitation or confusion on such open ground would probably be fatal in a firefight. It was usually considered too dangerous to deploy in broad daylight.

Two team leaders coordinated communications, and drew a rough sketch of the compound on a scrap of white paper with a marker pen, which was passed around. This detailed potential entry and exit points. An arrow depicted the angle and direction of landing.

The rest was bedlam. As soon as we hit the ground, and sprinted down the ramp, we took fire from four or five separate locations. We dived for cover as best we could on what was a large, roughly farmed piece of scrubland, and the pilot had no option but to get out of Dodge. The nature of the mission had changed from a relatively straightforward vehicle restraint into a scary, full-frontal assault.

Some of us returned fire from a kneeling position, others let loose from a prone position. We couldn't retreat and regroup. We were in the line of fire, whether we wheeled right or left. There was no option but to advance in unison towards the compound, the longest 200 metres of my life away.

Shhhhiiiitttt . . .

I had my head down, firing. I tried to freeze my brain, but my anger simmered. They were trying to kill me and my mates. Our positions were raked by rounds from Chinese machine guns. Bullets pinged off the rocky surface, flicking dust into our faces and down our throats.

In extremis, you trust your training. The ground was soft, rutted, and difficult to negotiate, but we resorted to a basic combat drill: fire and manoeuvre. This involves rapid, highly coordinated movement:

one half of the unit delivers covering fire for the other half as it advances 15 metres or so, before roles are reversed and the group unites on a baseline before repeating the process.

The technique was thought to have been introduced by the Swedish king Gustavus Adolphus during the Thirty Years War against the Habsburgs, which ended in 1648. It was used during the First Boer War and led to what strategists regard as one of the most humiliating defeats in British military history, the Battle of Majuba Hill in February 1881.

As you can imagine, history wasn't exactly at the forefront of my mind at the time. It was only later that I realized that charging the enemy by running towards machine guns in fortified positions had echoes of the First World War. I am amazed more of us did not get hit, since we were hopelessly exposed.

For a 'What the fuck?' moment it took some beating.

Retreat was inconceivable, because running away would have surrendered our initiative, which was pretty limited in the first place. There was nowhere logical to run to. It would have got their tails up, and probably resulted in them swarming after us. At least by running at them and shooting back there was a chance they would panic.

As far as plans go, ours was to make them realize we meant business. That didn't involve screaming at them, which was what some people imagine we get up to in such circumstances; we were too busy trying to decipher radio messages to try the rebel yell trick. One minute I was running forward, eyeballing the enemy. The next I was flat on my back.

My first instinct was that I had tripped. I was, after all, hardly concentrating on planting my feet when I was scanning the compound walls. The adrenaline was flowing very fast, and I was hyper-focused. I wasn't in any pain. But, gradually gathering my senses on the ground, it felt as if I had been stung by a bee, or my arm had been brushed by a hot piece of metal.

I rolled over at the moment it was our turn to return fire. I gestured to Flo, one of my best mates, who was alongside me.

'I think I've been shot, mate.'

'Shut the fuck up, and don't stop until we're in that fucking building.'

There really was no answer to that.

It took a split second to convince myself that I was imagining my plight. Surely, I reasoned, if I had taken a bullet I would have known all about it. Once I was back in the zone I piled forward, firing and fighting until I reached the external wall of the compound, where we regrouped. The insurgents were making themselves scarce, and I was back in the old routine.

Surge round the corner, kick the door in, and away we go.

I don't want to belittle or challenge the emotions I expressed at the start of this chapter, because they run deep, but I'm sure you know what I mean when I say we cleared the building of the enemy.

It was only during a lull in the fighting that I realized I had this crimson stuff running off the end of my rifle. I lifted my right hand, my trigger hand, and it was soaked with blood. My sleeve was red and moist, from the shoulder down.

Oh, fuck . . .

I had been shot, right through the muscle at the top of my shoulder – a so-called million-dollar wound, because it was a passport home without being life-threatening. The bullet missed the bone completely. Thankfully it didn't hit an artery, because I would have bled out in the middle of the firefight. I had survived on adrenaline, anger and unquestioning faith in a friend.

The medic did the rest. He tore my sleeve off, applied a tourniquet, and bandaged the wound before giving me two tubes of hi-energy gel to spike my sugar levels, and a couple of litres of water. I sat down with as much dignity as I could muster, and promptly threw up.

Did the lads take the piss about me chundering on the job?

What do you think?

Benny, my sergeant major, saw through the joke. I insisted I wanted to fight on if the enemy retooled and returned under the cover of darkness. He was unequivocal: 'We have to casevac you, because you'd be a liability in another contact. I'm not taking the risk of us being cut off, and you being a distraction if you're sitting here pissing blood again.'

I knew, deep down, he was right to call in the standby Black Hawk. I jumped in the back, and resisted the American medic who was offering me a cocktail of drugs, including a Fentanyl lollipop, a lozenge on a stick used to control so-called breakthrough pain in cancer patients. It is reckoned to be between fifty and a hundred times stronger than morphine.

I didn't need that crap.

News of casualties in a firefight had evidently reached Camp Bastion, since when I arrived I was greeted by a group of about twenty doctors, nurses and orderlies who whipped me into the operating theatre. Their first thought was to clean the wound, but, embarrassed, I was in rufty-tufty mode and refused to have a local anaesthetic.

'Are you sure, mate?'

'Yeah, yeah. I'm cool.'

I changed my mind when they began to push a steel bottle brush, about a centimetre in diameter, through the wound to scour away any dead flesh, dirt or infections from the battlefield. As they dragged it back and forth, like a bootneck cleaning the barrel of his rifle, I hit the roof. I had never known such excruciating pain.

'Stop, stop, stop! Give me the anaesthetic.'

'We thought you'd say that.'

If that wasn't sufficiently surreal, some of the guys from the firefight marched into the operating theatre as I was lying on the table, being stitched up. They'd cleaned house in the compound, collected the weapons cache, and wanted to check up on me as soon as they returned.

Kind, eh?

Hmm . . .

They burst out laughing, and proceeded to take the piss. Instead of flowers, chocolates and a bottle of barley water for the wounded hero, they had brought a camera. I've still got the money shot of me, off my head, smiling manically with my good arm raised as I gave them a thumbs-up.

I suppose it was puppy love. I refused the immediate offer to return to the UK, to rest and recuperate, because I wanted to stay with my unit. I wouldn't even take their advice to give myself a chance to come down by staying in hospital for a couple of days. I discharged myself, headed for the airfield, told them who I was and where I needed to go.

As luck would have it, I hitched a lift on a Hercules which was just about to head for Kandahar. I was still recovering from the anaesthetic and had been pumped full of powerful antibiotics, so it was no surprise I fell asleep almost before we took off. I woke with a start when the plane landed and, still dazed, headed down the tailgate.

Where the hell was I? I didn't recognize the layout of the airfield, and asked the landie, the guy responsible for monitoring passengers and cargo, whether we had been directed towards a different part of the landing zone. He looked at me as if I was mad.

'We're in Kabul, mate.'

It turned out that I had missed my stop, like a drunken commuter on a late-night train. They didn't wake me in Kandahar because they assumed I had been reassigned to Afghanistan's capital city. Fortunately, they were returning immediately to Kandahar. I got back on with a significantly less inflated opinion of myself than when we'd left Bastion.

They didn't exactly have the bunting out when I returned to base. The lads ripped it out of me: 'You don't need to get shot if you want to be a celebrity . . . a shoulder scratch isn't going to get your dick sucked . . . too big-time for Bastion, eh?'

Sympathy was still in short supply when I immediately went down with chronic sickness and diarrhoea. If anything, this dose of so-called Afghan Flu was worse than the bug that had made life at FOB Inkerman such a misery for my Marines unit the previous year. The intravenous antibiotics had wiped out my immune system. Everything was coming out of both ends, at all times of day and night. I couldn't even stand up. Man, taking another bullet would have been a sweet relief.

I had a season ticket for the heads, so it was predictable that I would be on my knees, hunched over a toilet bowl, when the lads returned from a job in the early hours. They were heading noisily for the showers when they heard me retching, kicked the stall door open, and fell about laughing at the sight of me, white as a sheet and green around the gills.

God, I loved those guys. The problem was, I also felt their pain.

NINE

Dear Diary

FLO IS MY rock, my go-to man. He looked after me like a brother on the battlefield, and we've helped each other through life-changing injuries. It hasn't been easy, because his sacrifice has been substantial, but his strength of character and raw courage are inspirational. He will hate me saying this, but he is a hidden hero.

It is one of my biggest regrets that I was not there when he needed me most. I was in Kandahar, wallowing in the sleep-deprived misery of constant sickness and diarrhoea, when word filtered through that Flo had been shot in the face on an operation. The left side of his cheek and jaw had been destroyed. I felt a surge of guilt and a wave of nausea that owed nothing to a sustained bout of Afghan Flu.

I was devastated, bereft. What if I had been next to him, as he had been next to me during that assault a week or so previously? The least I could have done was tell him that he was not alone.

He is a special man. Just how special? Despite the horrific nature of his wounds, he walked unaided on and off the casevac helicopter, and into the operating theatre. He wanted to be fully aware of what was happening to him, so he refused all painkillers until he was put under, prior to surgery.

His plight took us all to a dark place in our psyche. Death, strangely, is almost more straightforward to deal with, because of its immediacy and finality. IEDs tear off limbs and, God forbid, reproductive organs, but acute facial injuries are a particularly haunting element of a soldier's nightmare, since they steal your self-esteem and change people's perception of you, so they see you as a victim.

Shrapnel and bullet injuries in the First World War led to the development of plastic surgery, through the pioneering work of Harold Gillies in facial reconstruction. It is now possible to transplant all or part of a victim's face, and techniques in repairing nerves and muscle function have improved enormously in recent years. Flo was eventually given a medical discharge from the unit after years spent in reconstructive surgery. There's not a scrap of shame in that, but he struggled with it, since his work as a senior elite soldier inevitably helped to define him. I no longer see the severity of his facial scarring, but strangers stare. Something as mercifully normal as dropping his kids off at school can be tricky.

Our friendship grew when we were both at our lowest ebb, around the camp at Poole, coming to terms with changed circumstances. We became extremely close, drinking and simply thinking. What was life all about? What had it given us, and what had it taken away? Those questions recur, to this day. All I know is that Flo is a strong man. He'll keep on keeping on.

Camaraderie is a very personal thing. The emotions expressed are meaningful. We don't want praise or public thanks, since that goes against the team's code, but I wanted to give you some idea of Flo's stature and personality because guys like him deserve recognition for who they are, and not merely for what they've done.

We're not robotic killing machines, pre-programmed to follow orders. We are normal human beings, with everyday problems. The difference, I suppose, is that we are striving for something more than an ordinary life. We want to make a difference. We have an obsessive drive to live life to the fullest. We've found what many of us didn't know we were looking for.

My friendship with Flo means more to me than the mention in despatches I received for gallantry or the medal quietly presented by the First Sea Lord. There are so many unwritten stories hinted at by the names on one of our most sacred shrines at the heart of the camp in Poole. The memorial to the guys lost on operational duty brings everything home.

When Flo was shot we were taking a lot of casualties. It was a really bad time. I hadn't realized how big an impact that was having, psychologically, until I retrieved two small notebooks with entries covering the month or so around my initial wounding and ultimate paralysis. They were in the bottom of a drawer, their black plastic covers still covered with a thin layer of dust from Afghanistan.

The diaries still speak to me. When you have been immobile for so long, you forget what it feels like to write something in your own hand. You even forget what it looks like, and how it is an undervalued form of self-expression. It's upsetting because it represents a closed-off choice. I no longer have the luxury of using fancy calligraphy, or yelling in block capitals, if the mood takes me.

Those two notebooks contained fragments of thoughts and feelings. One included algebraic equations, geometric principles and rough calculations: during downtime I was teaching a few of the senior lads the rudiments of mathematics, which came pretty easily to me, even during my haphazard days at school. They needed to pass the subject at A level at the end of the tour to gain promotion. I had to come across as being confident, because they would have eaten me alive if there was the slightest indication I was bullshitting. It was weirdly dislocating: we'd created a little classroom in the middle of nowhere, would deploy, do the business (some of us called it 'delivering the hard news'), and then, after a couple of hours' sleep, reconvene to learn that $5x - y = 15$.

How we bounced from aggression to contemplation without blinking, or our brains blowing up, is beyond me. Perhaps it served as a distraction from our demons. Everyone deals with them in their own way, some better than others. People see things from different perspectives, so it stands to reason events would affect them differently.

I found it liberating to put down on paper the thoughts that were smashing around my skull, because it gave me a little more clarity about some of the issues I was wrestling with. I deliberately disguised my script so that it was a barely intelligible scrawl. It might have been because I simply didn't want to risk embarrassment if anyone in the unit read it, but I suspect there was a deeper motive.

The bleakness of my mood was captured by a song I played incessantly at the time, 'One Last Breath' by Creed, a post-grunge American rock band that sold more than fifty million albums, worldwide, before going into hibernation in 2012. The opening verse and chorus, describing the bleakness of someone facing their final moment, seemed horribly relevant.

I was secretly sensitive about how much we all had to lose. Being shot had obviously shaken me up mentally, more than I let on. I was preoccupied by my mortality. The questions I asked myself, as I sat alone, writing, listening to emotionally charged music and waiting for the go call, grew increasingly profound.

What will my last moments be like? What am I doing on this planet? What is my purpose? Is this my purpose? Why are we all here? Am I supposed to know the answers to these questions? If not, who is going to give me them? If this is a journey, then where is the destination?

The thoughts were so distracted, so disturbing, I wondered what people would think if they read them after I'd gone. Would those diaries be my legacy, all that people knew of me? I didn't really want the world to know the horrible places my mind was taking me to, but my words gave me away.

Some didn't make a whole lot of sense – 'Hatred is fucked by the causes of war. It makes us reliant on control.' Others were in the form of song lyrics, which fascinate me because they say so much about the writer. If I was feeling clever I would even try to make them rhyme, in schoolboy fashion:

> How fucked up is this existence where we put up so much
> resistance.
> All striving for answers which none of us deserve.
> Maybe there's a reason we're not supposed to know.
> Just like the cleanliness of snow
> Too great for our minds to contemplate
> So we in turn get left to our fate.

I'd written 'truth' below that one, and signed it. Reading it again, all these years later, is dreamlike. I am instantly transported back to that bare room. I reimagine the musty smells, the muffled sounds filtering through thin, temporary walls. I can visualize the accommodation block so accurately it feels as if I am retracing my steps around it, without anyone noticing.

It is a snapshot in time. When you feel safe, with a nice little house, a circle of friends and new ambitions to engage you, it is easy to forget how vulnerable you are, or how precious life is. It is only when you have a near-death experience that you realize the perfect existence might be an illusion. It is impossible to put everything into perspective in one go.

Most of the guys were at least five or six years older than me, and had far more combat experience. They'd done their growing up. I wanted to get the inside scoop. I was fascinated by the unknown, how and why people reacted to certain situations. I wanted to serve in the SF because I knew I would be faced with things beyond the comprehension of the average person. I was striving for answers about life itself.

It was hectic, and a little confusing. I was trying to put trippy thoughts into words, and didn't understand the process because I didn't really understand myself. The snippets are deeply personal, and probably difficult to relate to, but they still speak to me.

The diaries mix the mystical, in the form of do-it-yourself psychology sessions, with the mundane – shopping lists that reminded me I needed shaving foam, a protein shaker, and to cash a cheque. Zeroing my rifle, cleaning my sights, was on another to-do list alongside sourcing a new pair of night vision goggles.

Reading those lists now makes me smile, because it reminds me I so loved the life. It gives me a sense of the young man I was before my injuries. I was proud. I felt a deep sense of happiness, almost indecent joy. But when I read on, and the mood dips sharply as my mental meandering intensifies, I wonder if I am deluding myself through a strange form of nostalgia:

I must by the end of this tour have found what I'm looking for. I think all this time searching the world for something to condemn or enlighten myself has been wasted. In some respects running or moving to new places to solve your problems can cause more complications. You end up chasing your own tail and not getting anywhere.

There's a lot to unpack there. It's a bit of a stream of consciousness, but I get from it a strong sense of emptiness. I was a global orphan. I would travel from place to place, country to country, but had no real home. Sure, I could have gone back to South Africa, but I'd seen that, done that. I needed to meet new people, experience different cultures. I needed to open my eyes. I'd seen and done a lot in my job without feeling I was getting anywhere in my journey through life. I was going around in circles. I wasn't meeting a burning desire to feel fulfilled. Frustration was seeping out of me. I was torn, struggling to work out who I was.

I know I'm not satisfied with my existence. It's like a virus or a cancer, eating at my very being. How to stop this, or change my mundane life? Why do I mess this up by not being satisfied with who I am? That is the bottom line and start point of all subsequent problems.

I then switched to capital letters, presumably for dramatic effect: 'NOT SATISFIED WITH WHO I AM AT THIS MOMENT.'

I had a version of this internal conversation with Ben, my brother, many times. I never wanted a boring life, or an easy life. I sure as shit didn't want that picture of the perfect wife, in the perfect house, in the perfect neighbourhood. I didn't want the comfort of nine-to-five, Monday to Friday, feet up in front of the TV with a cheeky beer or ten at the weekends.

I know this is a cliché, but you only have one life. I had a compulsion to drive myself to extremes. The irony was that when I achieved anything I still felt empty. I had this irritating inner voice, gnawing away, taunting me: 'Time is running down. Life is moving on. What are you doing with it?'

Mates would wonder what I was on about if I even hinted at a private struggle. They told me I was on another level. I was experiencing life on steroids. I had travelled around the world. I had pushed my mental and physical capabilities beyond those of 99.99 per cent of the population. Why on earth wouldn't I be happy?

Perhaps never being satisfied is a basic human instinct, a trait of high achievers. Is it my default setting? I was certainly swerving all over the road.

I need to be better than everyone. Everyone wants to be me and everyone must want me. I am very vain and I will do what it takes to become the centre point of everyone's lives.

What an arrogant little shit, I hear you say, thinking he is top dog. I'd better explain myself, because I come across as a narcissistic wanker. I was twenty-four. I wouldn't have reached the unit without supreme self-confidence, channelled in the right direction. I know I wrote those words, but I didn't really want to be admired, like some sort of god.

It's a disguised plea for help. I wanted to be accepted in life. I never had a father who accepted me. My mother kept her distance. I didn't accept myself. I was a loner, alone. It was me against the world, and I needed to win. I was searching for acceptance in some shape or form, and hoped I had finally found it in the military.

There's an old line about there being no atheists in a foxhole, but any of the lads who were religious tended to keep their beliefs to themselves. Our padre was a great bloke who offered a sounding board if required, but any spiritual thoughts tended to be intimate, private. Reading them, out of context, can be deceptive.

> It was as if life was too short for those who knew there was more to life than just living. It is a cruel irony that they are to know but will never know. Those who know will never know. Above and beyond the realm of earth, just like an astronaut.

I may come across as dazed and confused in that passage, but it dripped with hidden meaning because of the timing. I wrote it on returning from an operation in northern Afghanistan, which cost the life of a close friend.

John Harrison was a Scot who had been brought up in South Africa. He was five years older than me, but we bonded immediately as gym buddies when, as an outstanding member of the Parachute

Regiment, he was assigned to Kandahar. He was a great lad, resourceful, self-effacing and funny. He fitted in perfectly.

He died instantly when he was shot in the head soon after we landed. We retrieved his body from the battlefield; it lay, covered with a sheet to preserve his dignity, on the floor of the helicopter transporting us back to base. To be in such close proximity to him, remembering the conversations we had a few hours earlier, pierced the heart.

I was upset, angry, grieving, questioning. That diary entry reflected my struggle to make sense of it all. One moment John was there, the next he was not. His body was there, in front of me, but where had he gone? Did he know where he was? Was he up there, looking down on earth like an astronaut? He'll never be able to explain.

Looking back, calmly and with the perspective provided by the passage of time, it was a highly charged reflection of the intensity and turmoil of such a major operation, which required the go-ahead from the highest levels of government.

It was a dark night, which gave the surrounding mountain range a bottle-blue hue. We flew low, into chaos, on twin-engined American Boeing CH-47 Chinooks, which laced the landing area with defensive fire while trying to evade rocket-propelled grenades, the red glow of tracer bullets, and rounds from all directions.

Everything happened so fast. John was hit almost as soon as we ran off the tailgate. The compound, a maze of small rooms, was heavily fortified; insurgents were firing from the roof, the base of the walls and the surrounding scrubland. We went in hard and fast, and I provided covering fire into enemy positions.

Once the aim of the mission had been achieved, we had a duty to recover John's body, irrespective of whether that involved more casualties. He was a big lad who weighed around 110 kilos with his kit on. We transferred him from a ditch and strapped him on to a stretcher. Though the medics told us he had gone, we couldn't quite believe it; in any case we were going to be respectful to his remains.

It was bedlam. Radios blared with people calling in the casevac, and screaming about the direction of incoming fire. Explosions lit up the night sky. Five of us had the responsibility of bringing John home, four bearers and a front man, who covered the others in addition to acting as a guide. We had to cover 600 metres to reach the landing zone, behind some trees, running at full tilt over rocks, through muddy irrigation ditches and cornfields. We had to trust our instincts, since if one man tripped we were all in the shit. Exhaustion set in as our adrenal glands ran out of juice. We rotated the stretcher if one of us flagged. My thighs were burning, but it was as if I was consumed by some unseen force. I was going to get the job done regardless because that was the least I owed John and my comrades.

I was not going to be the weak link in the chain.

I'm still in touch with John's parents. I hope I managed to pass on how much he meant to us, and that their visit, to see his name on our memorial, provided a measure of solace. His repatriation service stays with me. We wore our berets in his honour, and stood to attention, tears running down stern faces that masked our sorrow.

I still well up every time I hear a bugle playing the Last Post, because it summons the indelible image of his coffin, draped in the Union flag, being borne into the back of a Hercules. I tried to articulate my feelings, after saying farewell to John in a sombre silence that was almost too much to bear, but came up empty:

Writing again just to pass the time I guess, I'm struggling to put my thoughts into words. I think it's because I don't quite know what to say.

I don't say this lightly, and I don't want this to be misconstrued, but looking back now, I would have been OK with being killed in battle, fighting for a cause. I always wanted an honourable death. I still do. I don't want to pass away in some hospice, helpless and incontinent. That lack of dignity and control scares me.

The last four words I put down on the page, before I was paralysed, unwittingly sum up everything I try to do today, more than twelve years on. They nudge me, tease me. Perhaps on some level I knew what was coming – the greatest challenge of my life. Maybe we should all pay closer attention to those four little words:

Don't worry. Be happy.

LIFE TWO

TEN

Coming Up for Air

I HAVE BEEN manipulated on to my side. I'm still in a neck brace, but the tube draining spinal fluid from the back of my head has been detached. The doctors' next task is to remove the fifty-one staples around the base of my skull, linking entry wound to exit wound. I feel pressure, a tugging action, but no pain. The noise, though, is terrifying.

Ting . . . ting . . . ting . . . ting . . .

I obviously can't see anything, and my imagination is running wild, because those staples are effectively keeping my head on my shoulders. I am listening to them drop into a glass bowl as they are pulled out. It's a tinny, haunting sound, a bit like a chime from a cheap carriage clock. I try to speak, but nothing comes out. Not even a croak.

I've had a cuffed tracheostomy. Essentially that involves a balloon, attached to the tube inserted into my throat, being inflated so it seals against the inside walls of the airway. That ensures the air from my ventilator enters the lungs and is expelled via an insulation port on the tube, rather than my nose or mouth. It doesn't pass over the vocal cords, so I'm mute.

The only noise I can make is a sort of click, with my tongue. I don't know if I will be able to talk again. I'm also petrified that the ventilator could pop out when I'm alone. I can't call for help. All I can do is click. That's a bloody scary prospect when you're flat on your back, immobile, and your field of vision is a small patch of ceiling.

You can't turn your head, left or right, to check if anyone is around. Who is there? Someone? Anyone? Panic sets in. I'm screaming inside. How can I communicate, if my words are imprisoned in my mind?

Compared to today's advances, in which researchers register the brain waves of paralysed patients who are unable to speak so they can turn what they intended to say into sentences on a computer screen, we were in the Stone Age.

Occupational therapists at the Queen Elizabeth Hospital in Birmingham, helped by my brother Ben, used a crude communication tool, a square wooden board on which were groups of letters, in alphabetical order, in four quadrants. They would read my eyes as I flicked to a particular quadrant, and narrowed it down from there. When they got it right I either nodded, or blinked.

It took up to twenty minutes for them to decipher my thoughts and read a word back to me. They told me not to worry, that the process would accelerate, but I'd had enough. I didn't go back to the board to reinforce the point, but I made it clear that I wanted them out of my face. I couldn't deal with being in the emotional cement mixer any longer.

I was desperately thirsty and acting unpredictably, since I was in the early stages of being weaned off powerful sedatives. I tried to mumble, but could only mouth a single word: 'juice, juice, juice'.

Why I didn't simplify that, and ask for water, is beyond me. It was only when Ben read my eyes, and then my lips, that he realized what I wanted.

Someone grabbed a plastic cup containing orange juice, and gave me a sip. It scoured the back of my throat but felt like a crystal clear stream. The nurses quickly realized I was severely dehydrated, and hooked me up to an intravenous saline drip. Would this be my life from now on, a sequence of misunderstandings and crises of various magnitudes?

I was still untying the knots in my brain, but the future felt bleak. I didn't know it at the time, because I was still largely out of it, but the only source of positivity was my patient's diary, a laminated book on the front of which the hospital crest was emblazoned. It contained a stark description of my hour-by-hour status in the intensive ther-apy unit in those early days, when I was clinging to life.

Mum and Ben had been briefed by the Defence Medical Welfare team on arrival. A dispassionate list of priorities – ventilation, sed-ation, brain scans, angiograms, surgeries and bone grafts – hinted at the odds stacked against me surviving. One of Mum's entries cap-tured me as a tortured soul: 'Bad hallucinations and paranoia. Tried to reassure you, but it didn't work.'

That line brings it all back. I'm fearful, floundering, lost in a fog.

It's also hugely emotional to return to the visitors' book, covering the first couple of weeks in an observation room before I was trans-ferred to a bare basement ward: 'Hang in there, Tobz, we are all thinking of you . . . You are a true fighter . . . Your strength and cour-age are an inspiration to us all . . . I'm here for you, always will be, no matter what . . . Stay strong, the lads will always be there for you . . .'

The names alongside the inscriptions make me smile. Knowlesy, Aiden, Smudge, Sponge, Mudders, Starkie – comrades in arms, from Lympstone, Faslane and the Sangin Valley. Flo, in the early stages of his rehabilitation, was one of my first visitors, his damaged head in a protective cage. That last message was from my regimental sergeant major, who talked me down when I was at my most paranoid, convinced I had been captured.

Going cold turkey, after being slowly eased out of my coma, was brutal. It was hard enough to rest in the neurological unit, because the lights were always on, but being deprived of sleeping medication tipped me over the edge. Consumed by cold sweats, I lost all rationality and succumbed to an addict's uncontrollable, indiscriminate anger.

I would have done anything to get the drugs that obliterated the pain, and sent me into a fuzzier, more soothing world. Unable to lash out physically, I screamed unintelligibly at the nurses. In the early stages of my recovery I had been put back under because doctors were worried I was a danger to myself; now, six weeks in, I wasn't given the option. I had to do it tough.

There were small signs of progress. The cuff on my tracheostomy was gradually lowered in hourly sequences, so doctors could monitor my oxygen saturation levels and see whether I could maintain the natural balance of gases in my blood. I used to yearn for the respite this gave me, and even began to make myself understood with the occasional word.

When the cuff was reinflated it drove me to despair. It felt as if I was being put back in a deep, dark box. Being silenced again, through no fault of my own, was horrible. Inside, I was yelling at the top of my lungs, but no one was listening. That's such a suppressive experience. I understand why the dispossessed feel alienated and frustrated.

It took years for me to make peace with myself. I couldn't see a light at the end of the tunnel for so long. It was as if I lacked shape and substance. I existed, but in what form? As a freak, an inanimate object, a figure to be pitied? I didn't see the point of going on. I just went through the motions, day by day. I couldn't bear to see even a week into the future. It was so depressing I couldn't face it.

Even royalty copped it. Prince Charles paid me a huge compliment by insisting on seeing me, though it meant going out of his way during a visit to the nearby military rehabilitation centre in Selly Oak. He was really warm and solicitous, thanking me for my service and my sacrifice in a manner that went beyond the usual formalities, but I was pretty sour. I told him all I wanted was the pen with which he signed the visitors' book. He laughed and refused, saying it was a gift, but obviously remembered the request. He brought it up when I met him again, at a reception at Windsor Castle several years later. He had obviously been briefed on my progress, but the pen was still off limits.

I was sustained by the devotion of strangers. The nurses who dealt with me were phenomenal. One in particular, a Filipino called Aristotle De La Cruz, was a lifesaver. It's the sort of name that stays with you; over time I habitually used it, in full, whenever we met. His delight when I did so was one of the few things that made me smile.

He cared for me at the lowest point, when I was at my most vulnerable. I was lying flat, staring at the ceiling for twelve hours at a time. The highlight of my day was being turned on my side periodically, so

the nurses could check for pressure sores and signs of skin degrad-
ation. My dignity had disappeared. Coming to terms with being
incontinent is hard to digest mentally, because it strips away any
sense of self-worth. Coming from my background, as someone who
prided himself on self-reliance and held his head high, it was hard to
accept I needed someone to wipe my arse. I'd had an operation to
insert a suprapubic catheter, a tube which goes through the stomach
wall into the bladder. The fact that you will be pissing into a bag,
strapped to your leg, for the rest of your life, is also hard to accept
when you are twenty-four.

Aristotle radiated goodness. He bathed me, cleaned me, shaved
me, spoon-fed me. I don't know whether he had any training for
my type of situation, but he just knew how to deal with it. He was
so warm, comforting and understanding, so human. His greatest
gift was the ability to avoid making me feel any lower than I already
felt.

I am forever in his debt. I know that is the sort of easy phrase that
people can trot out without truly buying into its meaning, but believe
me, that comes from the bottom of my heart. We lost contact, and I
often wonder where he is now. It would be lovely to learn that he
followed my advice, and joined the RAF. They were offering incen-
tives of up to £50,000 for the best-qualified nurses at the time, because
of staff shortages. Aristotle didn't want to go to war, and was scared
he would end up on the front line in Afghanistan, but I did my best
to convince him that was not how it worked. He would not be signing up to be a combat medic, a completely different role.

He gave me the softest landing possible from a series of hard
truths. I tried with increasing desperation to move my hands, arms

or legs, but could not detect even the slightest twitch. It was as if I had been turned to stone, and my brain couldn't deal with its betrayal by my body.

I can only speak for myself, but I've never reached the point of complete acceptance, which would feel like surrender. You learn to live with your immobility, but you never stop wanting, believing or trying. I don't wake up every morning and instinctively try to move, or fantasize that one day I'll be able to do so, but there is always a part of me that whispers, 'Maybe, just maybe, miracles can happen.'

That's when the logical side of my brain kicks in: 'Come on, Tobes. Let's just make the best of what we've got. Let's just give your life a point.'

Basic functions, such as eating, were reminders of new realities. I was initially fed through a peg-feed, a tube inserted directly into my stomach. It essentially acted as a large syringe, with liquid nutrients being pulsed through from a machine. It was a process of trial and error, because some paralysed patients can drown due to an inability to suck in fluid. That's checked using a dye, to see what muscles are being used in the act of swallowing.

Doctors were reluctant to allow me solid food, preferring to progress slowly from baby food to soup and energy-giving drinks and gels, but I eventually wore them down. My determination to try a pie for my first solid meal led to understandable concern, since a single undigested flake of pastry could have caused me to convulse, but I somehow brazened it out. I had three people hovering, ready to apply emergency procedures, as I had the first mouthful of this steak pie. I had never tasted anything so good. The flavour was so rich, so dense. The gravy felt like liquid velvet. It was amazing. Right there, in the middle of one of the weirdest scenes imaginable, I experienced my first flutter of hope.

It would take time, but I had the chance of eating normally, with assistance. That was a big tick. I'd discovered I could drink naturally, too. That was tick number two. I was in the process of learning to speak with greater clarity. That was the third tick. I'd also managed to move my head slightly. That was the fourth.

It wasn't much, but at least it was a gateway to a more tolerable existence.

Physiotherapy started as soon as I was responsive. The physios stimulated so-called passive movements, manipulating my legs, and bending my knees up to my chest. The next phase involved massaging my scar tissue with oils. It was a strangely sterile experience, since I had lost my sense of smell.

That will never return, because I cannot inhale through my nose. I can snort, and feel a pressure in my nostrils, and occasionally get a sense of an overwhelming fragrance when I'm somewhere like a hot kitchen, but simple pleasures, such as smelling a garden rose or a partner's perfume, are denied me.

Over time, other senses start to compensate. My sense of taste is more acute. The skin on my face is extremely delicate, so that shaving is pretty painful. If I go out in summer I have to be smeared in high-factor sun cream. My eyes are dry, but my ears are stimulated by the merest touch; if it is unexpected it almost sends me into spasm. My hearing is fine but my eyesight is getting worse, so that I need reading glasses. Welcome to middle age, kid.

I suppose it is as well that I have learned to cherish normality. That progression began around three months into my stay at QEH, after I had begged the nurses to take me outside. I was stuck in neuro ITU, without any form of natural light. My companions either died or were moved to other high-dependency wards. I hadn't seen the sky or felt the sun's rays since I was dragged away from that firefight in Afghanistan.

Granting that desperate wish was a long, involved process. Still flat on my back, I was attached to a portable ventilator. My bed was then wheeled into position, through double doors, to a fire escape which overlooked the car park. It was a freezing afternoon in late February, and the sensation of the cold, crisp air hitting my face was blissful.

It was overcast, but focusing on something more than 6 feet above me was a revelation. I could see the gentle movement of the clouds, and hear the hum of Birmingham's traffic. The ventilator ensured I couldn't speak, but I felt like screaming with joy. The nurses obviously sensed that, because they agreed to deflate my cuff. I whispered that I wanted to make a telephone call.

Sounds mad, doesn't it? Borrowing a mobile was hardly practical, but I had an overwhelming urge to share the experience with my childhood friend, Chris Webster, in South Africa. He picked up the call, but I was saying 'Chris, Chris, Chris' so softly he couldn't hear me. Understandably, he eventually rang off in confusion. I was sad, frustrated and dejected as they wheeled me back into my airless bay.

I had been reminded of life's small, simple pleasures before once again they were snatched away. We don't realize we take so much for granted until it is too late. It is unrealistic to expect people accustomed to so-called normality to relate to something so far outside their experience, but I guarantee that someone who has survived solitary confinement will understand what I'm on about.

I recently watched a new version of *Papillon*, the story of French convict Henri Charrière, who spent eight years on Devil's Island, enduring torture and self-isolation, before escaping. He didn't see a soul, and was not allowed to speak, yet never lost faith in the ideal of freedom. He would have been on my wavelength.

Such struggles are an object lesson in the power of human resilience. We were recommended to read a similarly incredible story during selection. *The Long Walk* tells of the escape from a Soviet gulag in northern Siberia by Slavomir Rawicz, a Polish cavalry officer captured by the Russians, and six companions in June 1941. Over the course of the next year they walked more than 2,000 miles to freedom in India. They evaded capture in sub-zero wastelands, and went for long spells without food and water. One fugitive died of heatstroke crossing the Gobi Desert and another perished after falling into a crevasse in the Himalayas with safety a matter of days away.

Slavomir told of being eventually assigned to a transit camp in Calcutta, before taking a troopship to the Middle East where he was reunited with Polish forces, and served in Iran and Palestine. He survived the Second World War, settled in Derbyshire, had five children and raised money for orphans. He died in 2004, aged eighty-eight, but left behind an enduring mystery.

The authenticity of his story has been challenged, without conclusive proof. But in a way, the truth is secondary to the symbolism of the tale, a powerful illustration of comradeship, collective trust, human endurance and ingenuity in adversity.

In the meantime, I had my own trials and tribulations to overcome. We're all human, and I suffer from horrible moments of depression, usually in the early hours, or when I am alone. But there's a bigger part of me that says I will not go gently into that good night. I want to be a beacon of positivity, and show what a human being can tolerate.

I believe in the virtues of the human spirit. I guess that is how ultimately I want people to see me, as someone whose spirit pushes him through the toughest times. Sometimes a blanket of doom folds over me, but as I've got older I've become better at coping. I hide the hurt from my friends, because I don't want them to see me upset.

I try to appear self-contained, but to be honest, it is often a facade.

There's an understandable misconception that a paralysed person cannot feel pain when, in fact, it is constant. Your body uses whatever means it can to tell you that something is very, very wrong. Even a wheelchair, which gives you a degree of freedom, means you are sitting in one position for hours at a time. The body is not designed to do that, and so it protests.

My carers can move me, shift the physical burden, but there is a price to be paid. The nerve pain is ever-present, a weird combination of fire and ice. The most recognizable comparison I can make is with a twisted, swollen ankle. The injury heats up, throbs constantly until it becomes difficult to bear, and periodically feels freezing.

The body is trying to tell the brain something is not right, but the signals are scrambled. It's that white noise you recoil from when you are trying to find the correct frequency on a radio dial. Through the confusion you hear echoes of the station you are looking for, but there's nothing substantial, just odd words, in an indecipherable language, that mean next to nothing. Your search must continue.

In that situation, all I can do is appreciate the little things. At

QEH that meant being introduced to a tilting frame, so I could sit up in bed and get my body accustomed to the consequent drop in blood pressure. That, in turn, led to being strapped into a standing frame, to check how I coped with being upright.

I did well, because I had retained a surprisingly good level of basic fitness, and my heart was really strong. I was also psychologically astute due to my military training, and applied myself mentally because I worked out that my blood pressure was one of the rare things I could control. I almost over-compensated by consciously raising my heart rate by working as hard as I possibly could to impress the doctors. That's difficult, because a paralysed person loses muscle tone and tension, but not impossible. I also worked on my neck movement, knowing that, if anything, it would get worse over time, because muscles stiffen and ligaments tighten. To move on, after nearly six months in limbo, I needed to give the doctors the impression of stability.

Instead, at the worst possible time, with enquiries being made about me being transferred to an intensive care unit in Salisbury to continue my rehabilitation, I contracted double pneumonia. I was very ill, and had to have both lungs continually evacuated in an unspeakably painful process that in layman's terms uses a specialized vacuum cleaner.

A suction pump is attached to a long thin straw, which is inserted into a port on the side of the tracheostomy and fed to the base of the lungs. Once in position, it sucks up mucus in intermittent bursts lasting between two and five seconds. The sound is grotesque, and the nerves spasm, which creates an excruciating cramp. It seems as if your entire body is in a state of shock.

It's very dangerous, too, since it has been known to induce heart failure, and there is only so much damage the delicate tissue within the lungs can absorb. Eventually the secretions are mixed with traces of blood shed by the trauma. You can see the tell-tale darkness in the bag collecting the waste matter, and it feels as if you are choking to death.

All you can think is 'Shit, I'm gonna die.' Preparing for the end is an unspoken ritual in intensive care in any case, but here it had a horrible immediacy. What will that last breath feel like? Have I made my peace with this world, and whatever comes later? Will I have the honourable death I crave? Am I going to be scared, or will I be calm?

Questions, questions. They recur, as weakness and illness recur.

I managed to recover from that bout of pneumonia so that once the call came through that there was a bed available in Salisbury I was discharged from QEH. I was put on a portable ventilator, carried into an ambulance, and set off on a three-hour journey with two nurses for company.

Feeling movement for the first time in what seemed for ever while obviously being unable to move was a surreal experience. I was strapped down for additional safety, facing the back of the ambulance, but couldn't see out of the windows since I was lying flat. Moving to a new hospital was a milestone, but my injury still felt like a millstone.

Florence Nightingale had a lifelong association with Salisbury, a large hospital that has served this lovely cathedral city in Wiltshire for 250 years. Typically for me, I quickly needed the urgent care of her successors, and the doctors in the ICU, because my pneumonia returned with a vengeance. Once again, I was put through the agonies of suction.

I was grey, suffering from cold sweats, and struggling to breathe. The doctors saw the discharge from my lungs, a familiarly horrible mixture of blood and dark green crud, and knew I couldn't take much more punishment. One tried to get a line into me, so I could receive intravenous antibiotics, but I was so swollen his search became increasingly desperate. Eventually, he found a vein in my foot.

I have a vivid memory of the horror on the face of my brother Ben as he was told the following twenty-four hours would be decisive. He was petrified, and promised he would stay with me throughout. That told me everything I needed to know. I was at death's door.

A fevered thought crossed my mind: *If I close my eyes, will they ever open again?*

ELEVEN

Windmills of the Mind

I OWE MY life to that doctor's persistence and professionalism. Without the antibiotics he forced into my system, that night would have been my last. If fate had been kind, I would have faded gently into unconsciousness and oblivion. The alternative, the convulsive terror of an increasingly hopeless fight for breath, doesn't bear thinking about.

The human body is a remarkable machine, even when most of its constituent parts don't work. Against the odds, once again, I gradually recovered. I was eventually transferred to a spinal ward, the closest I was going to get to normality for the next eleven months. The sense of release was immediate, but my relief was short-lived.

Even before I arrived in Salisbury, intensive-care staff had concerns about my state of mind. The drive for perfectionism that made me an over-achiever was being channelled negatively, so that I struggled to come to terms with the scope and pace of my recovery. Futility, a feeling I had previously refused to recognize, consumed me.

It seemed as if the nightmare would never end.

I was back in a small bay, stripped of privacy and staring at a different but equally soul-destroying patch of ceiling. It was a four-bed ward, and had that giveaway smell of well-diluted bleach and

overheated, recycled air. The milk of human kindness hadn't cur-
dled, because of the care lavished upon us in difficult circumstances,
but it was on the turn.

I was nearest to the nurses' station, which seemed like a cross
between a command post and a social centre. To my left, in a bed
closest to the window looking out on to a car park, where ambu-
lances queued to disgorge their damaged goods, was Mike. He had
hit a pothole on his bicycle and been thrown over the handlebars. He
snapped his neck when he buried his face into the road. He was in his
early fifties, and, like me, dependent on a ventilator. Ernie, a man in
his late seventies, lay opposite him. Already frail, he too had broken
his neck, when he fell down the stairs at home. Since the injury was
lower down his spinal cord, he at least had the release of being able
to breathe of his own volition.

The bed next to him was occupied sporadically by guys whose
injuries, while serious, were more manageable. Tim, a builder who
had broken his back after falling through a roof, recuperated for
about a month before being discharged. George, a young lad who
suffered a spinal injury playing rugby, also passed through.

We were all prisoners of circumstance, serving indeterminate
sentences. We chatted inconsequentially, as far as our mobility
allowed, without forming any real bonds. There is an inevitable self-
ishness involved in being a long-term patient, waiting and worrying.
To varying degrees, we all retreated into our own little worlds.

Hospital life went on around us. Despite the limitations of his
ventilation, Mike provided a running commentary on the sights and
sounds of the car park, where relatives competed frantically, and
occasionally comically, for space during visiting hours. I was more

conscious of the activity in the reception area to my right, where phones rang unanswered and nurses pored over seemingly endless paperwork.

The NHS is a brilliant institution, but it was impossible to ignore the fact it was fraying at the edges. The physios were in such demand they were unable to commit to the daily stretching sessions I felt I desperately needed. The nurses were short-staffed, and always seemed to be chasing the clock.

They cared, all right. But there was something impersonal, almost mechanical, about the way they would retrieve my wash bag from the small cupboard beside my bed and give me a bed bath each morning. It was pretty basic: they had a bowl of lukewarm water and a cloth, and proceeded to wash my bits. If I was lucky, and they had the time, they'd give me a shave.

They were a basic point of human contact, so I made a conscious attempt to get on well with them. It's like any enclosed relationship: there are some individuals you like, and others you're not so keen on. I had plenty of time to study their body language; I was drawn to those who were obviously sticklers for the little details. I saw a little bit of me in their irritation with the shortcomings of the system.

We were all playing a role, to an extent. The nurses made light of the pressure they were under, as if they were obliged to keep up the pretence of perfection. They had seen all sorts in their working lives, so they knew how to read people, especially when they were facing a personal crisis. I tried hard to be a cheeky chappie, but they probably saw through the facade.

Tears of a clown, and all that . . .

To tell the truth, I was worn down by the predictability of the routine. As the months wore on, I sensed increasing urgency from the welfare officers from the regiment, who were monitoring my progress. They understood I needed greater mental stimulation, and were worried that I was in the process of being institutionalized. Psychologically, my well-being was suffering.

There was, as usual, too much time to think. I brooded. Is this what the rest of my life is going to be like, cooped up in a hospital? Am I ever going to rejoin the outside world? I found it difficult to avoid recurring, disturbingly straightforward questions: Is it worth carrying on? Is there any point when the quality of my life is so poor?

It's not the sort of dilemma you can throw into a casual conversation, so I never discovered if the other guys in the ward felt the same way. I often wondered what was going through their minds as they drifted off into their private universes. One by one, they filtered back into society. Mike was the last of the regulars to leave; we lost contact, but I heard he ended up on the Isle of Wight.

Illogically, since medical decisions concerning other patients obviously never factored in my needs and sensitivities, I felt abandoned. I was the runt of the litter at the pet rescue centre, pining for a new owner who might never come. I took my pleasure where I could, particularly when that meant ending a six-month wait for my first shower.

It took so long to arrange because of a typical mixture of clinical caution and bureaucracy. Health and safety regulations, covering infection control, meant that each individual had to be allocated a personal shower chair. These could only be ordered from the central stores of an internal agency, which didn't exactly radiate urgency in terms of customer service.

Even then, I had to do a bit of negotiating with the staff who wheeled me into the wide, white-tiled shower room. They were reluctant to spray water directly on to my face because they didn't want to compromise my tracheostomy tube, but I pleaded with them to tilt my shower chair slightly backwards, so that I could feel the full benefit of yet another thing I had once taken for granted.

The sensation of being hosed down with a hand-held shower was amazing, absolute bliss. I had no feeling in most of my body, and (probably mercifully) my sense of smell was severely limited, so I almost had to imagine the cleansing effect. But when the water cascaded on to my head and face, I knew all about it.

I narrowed my eyes, but wanted to keep them open, almost to count the droplets on my skin. I didn't want it to end, but when it did I felt so refreshed. Mentally, it gave me an extended lease of life. It was as if a little bit of the old me, helpless, grubby and isolated, had been washed down the plughole, to be replaced by a shiny new model.

I was slowly adapting to a new identity as a quadriplegic. That meant coming to terms with a motorized wheelchair, a psychological challenge that took me by surprise. I formed a love–hate relationship with it; I was undecided whether it was my friend, or my jailer. On the one hand I saw it as a symbol of my disability. On the other, it was a fantastic source of freedom; without it I would have been stuck in bed all day.

Looking back, I was still going through a grieving process. My life had changed in an instant, leaving me alone in a world of unexpected obstacles. I wanted everything to be perfect because of my relative helplessness. Every tiny electrical malfunction would drive me nuts, since, to my mind, the chair emphasized my fragility, and played up to the prejudices of those who had no conception of my character or condition.

Dealing with pain and other physiological complications was pretty simple, partly because it was unavoidable. The psychological challenge was harder to deal with. I kept myself tight, emotionally. If I had private perceptions of uselessness – and they did exist – I kept them to myself. The body has no real outlet to fight paralysis, but the mind actively resists it.

Even today, I am able-bodied in 99 per cent of my dreams. Sleep is a refuge of normality. In my subconscious I'm still running, jumping, dancing, moving, but when I wake I am confronted with the reality that I have almost forgotten how to do those things. It is a gut punch that loses none of its ferocity through regularity.

The windmills of the mind whir incessantly, but there's no alternative but to take a deep breath and regroup. You have to stay grounded, remind yourself continually about the fallacy of the miracle cure. I realize I touched on the peril of false hope earlier in this book, but for the sake of anyone who finds themselves in a similar situation to me, I want to reinforce the dangers.

There is so much bullshit out there, designed to prey on your desperation. Don't get sucked into the mythology of medical science that there is a wonder cure just waiting to be discovered and exploited. I've seen people throw away their life savings chasing an unrealizable dream of regaining a degree of movement in their body. One guy I know went to China to have stem cells injected into his neck in some sort of crazy experiment. There's no proper science behind such schemes, which lack official recognition. They're bloody dangerous. I'm not saying that hope should be abandoned, since time moves on, and science progresses with it, but don't get lost in the fog of fairy tales.

Accept that this is it. Make the best of what you have got. Don't torment yourself. If a research scientist makes a breakthrough you will know about it very quickly.

There are wearable robotic exoskeleton suits on the market that enable individuals with spinal cord injury to stand upright, walk, turn, climb and descend stairs through the induced motion of hip and knee. They cost around £70,000, and are unsuitable for anyone with my degree of injury, because the makers assume you are able to use crutches. Other products stimulate muscles and nerves electrically. They can theoretically improve sleep, assist pain relief, and reduce reliance on medication. But forget the image of you being eased into some sort of bionic contraption capable of getting you running or lifting weights. That's just silly talk, and silly talk wrecks lives.

I left Salisbury with a clear-eyed understanding of my limitations. Improving my range of movement was probably beyond me. Preserving it for as long as possible was my aim. That involved a structured programme, concentrating on maintaining muscle mass and movement in my joints, which would otherwise start to seize up.

Without due care and attention, muscles atrophy. Pressure sores multiply and worsen. Skin, already sensitive to the ageing process, starts to degrade. It becomes perilously thin, which is extremely dangerous, because wounds never truly heal. Once skin tone breaks down completely, you are prone to infection, which seeps into the blood.

When that happens, the consequences are invariably fatal. There was no more poignant or symbolic victim than Christopher Reeve, who played Superman in four movies. An infected pressure ulcer caused a recurrence of sepsis, and led to his death, following a cardiac arrest, at the age of fifty-two in October 2004. At the time I was conscious of his passing only because of his star status. It was only when I sustained similar injuries that I was struck by the warning he delivered from beyond the grave.

Like me, he sustained catastrophic damage to his first and second vertebrae, in his case caused by being thrown forward from a horse and on to his head in May 1995. Like me, he stopped breathing for several minutes. Like me, he was saved by medics who bagged him, to force air into his lungs. Like me, he was heavily sedated and delirious in hospital. Like me, he was paralysed from the neck down and required a ventilator, but escaped brain damage. His life-saving surgery was a little more intricate, but equally invasive. Doctors used bone from his hip to act as a bridge between his top two vertebrae. A titanium pin was inserted and a hole was drilled through his skull, which was secured to the spinal column by fused wires. A charitable foundation in his name, and that of his late wife Dana, continues to study spinal injuries and conduct human embryonic stem cell research.

Reeve remained relentlessly positive in public, though I do not doubt he had his moments of private despair. Trust me. I know how easy it is to become depressed. It is a constant battle between light and shade. I've learned, the hard way, that a bad state of mind helps no one. Measured optimism is another key to relative longevity.

Accept that the future stretches before you, though it seems forbidding and uncertain. Accentuate the positive. Keep doing whatever exercise you can. Watch what you eat, because you can't shift weight once it piles on. Remain hydrated, because fluids help to keep the bladder healthy. Take advice on the right nutrients, and the best diet. Embrace your faults, and respond to them. No one is perfect. I probably don't do enough physio, though I have daily hour-long sessions concentrating on muscle stimulation and passive movement stretches that prevent my joints, ankles and fingers from locking up.

I am also a great believer in the healing power of hydrotherapy. I am hoisted into the water, which is heated to just below body temperature, between 34°C and 35.5°C. This enables muscles to relax and eases joint pain. My ventilator is detached from my wheelchair, placed on the side of the pool, and tended by my ITU nurse and carer. Two physiotherapists are in the water with me. I'm on my back, and feel weightless, so I can do certain stretches that are beyond me in the chair, or in bed. The physios hold me around my arms and allow my body to make passive movements. Think of the way aquatic plants move with the ebb and flow of tidal currents, and you will understand why they call the process 'seaweeding'.

It's uniquely relaxing and, crucially, gives me a huge sense of achievement and independence. This is a personal opinion, shaped by years of struggle balanced by minor triumphs of will, but I don't see how you can have a fulfilling life without keeping mind, body and soul healthy and intact.

I'm by no means an expert on the subject, but I believe passionately in the long-term benefits of mental stimulation. In my sort of situation it is critical to keep the mind sharp and active. I play a lot of chess and memory games. I try to read, listen to audiobooks and a range of podcasts. It's important to keep myself educated, worldly wise.

We all need friends. I was introduced to one of my best mates at the Recovery Centre hosted by the Help for Heroes charity at Ted-worth House, just outside Salisbury. It was my halfway house between hospital and returning to camp life in Poole; Headley Court, the main military rehabilitation complex near Epsom, in Surrey, couldn't take me because I was ventilated.

Tedworth House caters for wounded veterans and their families. Their programmes, which migrated online temporarily during the pandemic, operate on the principles of hope, control and opportunity. They put me in touch with Canine Partners, an amazing charity that provides assistance dogs who can do everything from putting your debit card into a cashpoint to opening doors or operating lifts.

Pets have become attuned to human emotion and patterns of behaviour during the evolutionary process. Dogs, for example, interpret tone of voice and body language. They understand many of the words we use, and look into our eyes to gauge our mood. Their loyalty is reassuring; they can reduce stress, ease depression, combat loneliness, and encourage exercise. A research study found they even increased the attention spans of children with ADHD.

I've always loved animals, and am a passionate supporter of rhino conservation programmes; despite their size and strength their vulnerability appeals to me. More conventionally, I grew up with dogs in South Africa, where pets also provided a form of personal security. I was on their wavelength, man and boy, so when Canine Partners, who help multiple sclerosis sufferers and stroke victims among others, offered to provide a companion, I seized the chance. In order to develop a special type of relationship, non-verbal but intimate, they sought to match me with a dog that had a complementary character.

I was looking for a free spirit, a dog with a gleam in its eyes. I didn't mind mischief; to be honest, I expected and encouraged it. Maybe, on some level, I knew the partnership would help to raise my spirits. After all, it was my responsibility to care for my new companion. With the best will in the world that was a real attraction, a nice change from being the one who was looked after.

The pairing process was delicate, and took time to succeed. Several dogs came to meet me, but never seemed to be the right fit. They tended to be quite skittish, mainly because of the hissing noise made by my ventilator. They were spooked by something that was obviously outside their frame of reference, so our speed dates came to nothing.

Wogan was different. A long-haired cross between a Labrador and retriever, he announced himself by shooting out of his cage at the back of the delivery van and racing around the grounds of Tedworth House, without an apparent care in the world. As his handlers struggled to corral him, he was evidently having the best day of his young life. So much for the advance notices of a well-trained, impeccably behaved dog, aged sixteen months, who had been in the system since he was seven weeks old. I was sitting on a nearby embankment, chuckling at his antics, when they managed to get him on the lead. He spotted me, pulled at the restraint, and ran towards me when he was, once again, set free.

I half expected him to lunge joyfully at me, but he stopped as he reached my wheelchair before deliberately planting his front paws on my lap. He wasn't fazed by the noise of the ventilator, and I was struck by his inquisitive look and boyish nature. It was as if he was saying to me: 'Who are you, then? What are you all about? Why aren't you stroking me? Why aren't you touching me? Come on. Play with me.'

It was love at first sight. We were a match made in heaven.

I didn't name him, though. Terry Wogan, the TV personality who had sponsored his training, had asked that he be named after him. In a way that was appropriate, because my new pal was a showman, with genuine star quality. He quickly learned to play to the crowd, and developed a range of party tricks that turned him into a local celebrity. He loved stealing the hat off my head, and the scarf from around my shoulders. He had the gentle touch of a pickpocket.

Once I was rehoused, in a small two-storey billet in the married quarters just outside the camp, he was desperate to go out and explore. That helped me through an unhappy, increasingly distressing time, because he represented a fragment of normality in an abnormal situation. He was boisterous, and charming. He helped me to get out of the house, and out of myself.

He saved my life, figuratively and factually.

In a philosophical sense, he gave me something to live for, something to get out of bed for. I fed off his energy. We were mirror images of each other; in some weird way he reminded me of who I had been, and who I could still be. He had a zest for life that was infectious. He combined cheekiness with cleverness. He knew when to play up and when to buckle down.

He recognized that, with me, he could get away with being naughty. He also understood that when his trainers arrived, to make periodic assessments of his suitability, he had to be on his best behaviour. It was uncanny; the moment they left he headed for his favourite gap in the fence, and was gone. He was how I imagined myself to be, a wild child with a good heart.

He also knew his own mind. He used to flatter some visitors by playing up to them, and would push the boundaries with others. If he didn't want to do something he turned to stone. One of my friends used to come on Tuesdays and Thursdays with the intention of giving him extra exercise, only to discover Wogan was having none of it. He was a big dog, around 35 kilograms when fully mature; he lay down and simply refused to move.

He was also trained to detect danger. On two separate occasions, when my personal care was so haphazard I was not being looked after properly, he literally saved my life. In both cases I had been left alone in a ground-floor room. My tracheostomy tube became detached, so I was unable to breathe. Without mechanical assistance, I have around ninety seconds before I pass out, and pass away. Wogan intuitively understood my distress, and my need for immediate help. He leapt at a red buzzer on the wall, which he pressed with his nose. Alarms sounded, he raced around the house, and, mercifully, staff came to my aid. Without his actions, I would have died.

I feel blessed to have shared my life with him for more than eight years, and have yet to fully get over his death, aged ten, in December 2018. I was devastated and guilt-ridden, because I was away at the time. The circumstances were inconclusive, but it seems he followed the Labrador's instinct to scavenge, and ate a poisoned rat, most probably left in the forest by those trying to cull local foxes.

I have seen a lot of death in my life, often in horrible circumstances, but the loss of Wogan, who slipped away during the night, affected me deeply. I try to smile when I remember him, but he had so much more to live for. Why did I take it so hard? I suppose it was due to his genuine nature. There was something about him that was so consoling.

Dogs love you, no matter what. That love is unconditional, non-judgemental. Human beings, on the other hand, are habitually cruel. They can be malicious to one another, often for the flimsiest of reasons or the most misguided cause. Wogan was there for me when I needed him most.

Boy, did I need him.

TWELVE

Walking Towards the Light

From: Commanding Officer

Toby,

Thank you for taking the time to meet me the other day. I hope
that in my role as CO, SBS, I can be of service and help you in any
way that I am able.

   When you joined the unit you joined a tight-knit family; you
remain a member of that family and as its head, for the time that I
am in command, my door is always open to you.

   I expect that the immediate team around you will help you
through the regular challenges that you face; however, when those
challenges appear unsurmountable, remember to draw your family
in close for support.

   I look forward to seeing you again soon.

I suppose we are all conditioned to making light of problems in the
face of authority. How many times do we tell the harsh truth when
someone we respect asks us how we are? Seldom, since a mixture of
false pride and common courtesy prevents us from unburdening
ourselves on a well-intentioned friend.

I was urged to tell my former CO, whom I obviously cannot name, how low I felt. Yet I knew his supportive words were far from empty. He was caring, considerate, and conscious of the powerful bonds that united the men under his command. Out of reciprocal loyalty, I chose the easy option of reassuring stoicism and superficial optimism.

It might have been best for both of us had I been more open about the depth of my depression. It could have given him additional impetus to challenge the restraints of the system. The unpalatable fact was that, instead of returning to camp being a release after seventeen months in hospital, it felt like an extension of an ordeal.

Strings had been pulled in the spirit of the SBS looking after one of its own. A semi-detached house, in married quarters close to the base, had been specially adapted, initially for an amputee, Terry, who had gone on to qualify as a helicopter pilot. An occupational therapist redesigned the layout of the ground floor, so that it was open-plan, with a bed, kitchen and living area.

It was designed as a temporary solution, until I could find a home of my own, which proved more difficult than anticipated. It wasn't perfect, since the upper floor was inaccessible, but it would have been manageable in different circumstances. As it was, I felt as if I was an imposition. I was back in a military environment, but as a spectator, rather than a participant.

The welfare team on camp sensed my unease, and were nervous about letting the lads see me. I understood why, since the irony of the situation was obvious: I badly missed the to-and-fro of active service, but operational gossip and the day-to-day routine of pre-deployment preparation merely emphasized my isolation.

Was I their worst nightmare, a constant reminder of their mortality? Was I in the way?

Don't get me wrong. I had good friends, doing their best for me. Flo had his own issues, but he was a rock. Paddy, who took shrapnel in the leg and fractured a knee cap in the daytime assault in which I was shot through the arm, worked from outside the system, since he had left the regiment to return to civilian life.

Thoughtful gestures meant a lot. The lads bought me an iPad, set it up on a table next to the bed, filled it with my favourite audiobooks and music, and arranged for someone to come in and connect everything up. I wasn't aware of it at the time, but they also clubbed together to buy me a standing frame, which offered a modicum of freedom.

That frame symbolized everything that was going wrong, because I had no control over the standard of external care I was receiving. It was so poor that my first set of nurses failed to notice that the frame was calibrated for someone 5ft 2in in height. I was 5ft 10½in, so although I loved being vertical, it was doing more harm than good.

Enter Jim Patrick, retired naval officer and chairman of the SBS Association, which provides holistic support to veterans. He saw the problem straight away. Responsibility for my medical care lay with the NHS which, in its cash-strapped state, opted for the lowest common denominator. Predictably, that posed questions about the quality of staff they were able to recruit. Everyone was stuck in their own silos.

Their computers said no.

I am fortunate today in having a brilliant care team, the seventh employed on my behalf since my injuries. The system operates collectively to meet my needs. It doesn't impose upon me, but is always there for me. Jim works proactively, coordinating a range of individuals and organizations on my behalf. I have all the support I need. I control it, rather than it controlling me. I feel enabled, and fulfilled.

The contrast with the first couple of years, marooned in married quarters, is scary. My decline was gradual, but could easily have been terminal. I was not being looked after properly, psychologically or physically. I was trying to figure it all out, almost learning how to be paralysed. I still had the urge to do the things I did as an able-bodied man; each realization of my limitations eroded my spirit, like water dripping continually on to stone.

Nothing was straightforward. I yearned for the rough and tumble of military routine. I could no longer go out for a spontaneous piss-up with my mates. Through no fault of their own, they were in a world that was visible to me, but tantalizingly out of reach. I lost count of the long, lonely nights of the soul where I lay there and relived my life in a series of freeze-frame images.

The kid in the bush, doing wheelies on his bike. The teenaged wild child, driving teachers to despair. The bootneck hitting the pub next to the station and disturbing the gentility of Exmouth, a seaside resort stuck in a fifties timewarp. The SF soldier who knew, from the look in a mate's eyes, that their secrets were special and, above all, safe.

They were all manifestations of me, but strangers, ghosts. When you are flat on your back, unable to move, it dawns on you that your life is very, very different. Your brain struggles to compute the enormity of the change. It doesn't implode, suddenly and dramatically, but your thoughts become fuzzy and indistinct.

It's strange. I wasn't aware of my decline as much as I should have been. Looking back, I see massive red flags, but at the time I was beaten down, conditioned to pain and disappointment. When you are at the dark heart of the struggle, living the problems, being bombarded by damaging emotions, you are blind to the dangers.

I was lost. I would be levered into my chair after breakfast and stare out of the windows all day. I would be vaguely aware of familiar sights, of lads coming back from a training run or an exercise, but it was as if they were blurred, at the edge of my field of vision. Imagine being forcibly retired, but still turning up at work every day. That's basically what was happening. I was there, but I wasn't.

I wouldn't say anything. I didn't want to talk to anyone. It was as if my brain couldn't accept things as they were, so it shut itself off. The mind protects itself by closing down. I was in a perilous place, and people were very worried about me. I had no hope, no direction, no energy, no sense of identity. Time lost its meaning as I sat there, like a zombie, for eight or nine hours at a stretch.

Before I knew it, it was time for me to be put back into bed. The lights would be turned off and I would struggle to sleep. The carers would retreat upstairs, as if I was an inconvenience. As my eyes adjusted to the darkness, and the silhouettes of basic necessities, scattered around me, emerged, I became increasingly conscious of their idle chatter and laughter. I was achingly lonely.

All I had to look forward to was waking up, after yet another disturbed night, and doing it all again.

There's a replica Olympic torch in my office, which reminds me of how far I had fallen. I carried it in my wheelchair on the Portland Bill to Bournemouth leg of the relay leading up to the 2012 Olympics, but was so depressed I cared nothing for the honour or the occasion. The mood was buoyant and celebratory, but all I could do was cringe with embarrassment. Sullen and self-pitying, I shuddered to think what the crowds were making of this helpless, heavily medicated young man.

Jim's perspective, and his protective nature, saved me. He recognized my distress, and investigated the shortcomings of the care agency that had won the tender for my contract from the NHS commissioning body. He was astonished and angered by the lack of due diligence, which undermined the good intentions of the MoD, his organization, and the SBS itself.

The desire to help me was genuine, but the lack of an overarching system meant I was in danger of falling between the cracks. To give a specific example, as a serving soldier I came under the auspices of the principal medical officer in the camp. But when I was discharged from hospital I was enrolled with the local GP, because I required additional medication.

That's fine, until convention confuses the situation. The GP, thinking I was still under military care, took delivery of my medical records but assumed he had no role to play. The PMO, aware that I had enrolled with the GP, assumed the NHS had undertaken responsibility to provide my primary care. The end result, until the impasse was solved, was that no one was looking after me.

The clinical care assessment dictated that I needed two carers, twenty-four hours a day. It was essential they were within thirty seconds of me, to deal with any unexpected calamity. It transpired that my first set of carers were untrained. Though nurses in their countries of origin, they lacked the qualifications to work in the UK care system. My physiotherapy was inadequate.

There was no consistency or accountability. People turned up on an ad hoc basis, with no apparent knowledge of the complexity of my condition. I had to tell them what to do, how to do it, and why they needed to do it. The contrast with my world, where orders were assimilated and carried out with maximum efficiency, was mind-blowing.

I regularly had strangers come to my door and announce they would be my overnight carer. Some were barely out of their teens, and others could barely speak English. One proudly admitted his area of expertise was caring for senior citizens. I had no option but to trust my life to them. Try dropping off to sleep with the knowledge that if anything happened to my ventilator, they were unlikely to react in time.

The principal nurse, in nominal charge of a team largely made up of Russians, Belarusians and Estonians, lived in Cheltenham, 130 miles away. She faced a five-hour round trip when she visited, once a month. The administrator, who was supposed to address organizational issues, also came once a month. There was no team leader, with daily oversight of problems.

It was a bureaucratic nightmare. I had to be home at 7 p.m., when staff changed over, so I had no social life to speak of. When it suited them, they were sticklers for the rules. That meant, for instance, that Jim often had to pick up prescriptions for me, because one carer refused to leave the other, even for the briefest period.

On one occasion, I was suffering from a bad chest infection. The pharmacy couldn't deliver the medication, and Jim was away on business. The carers got me out of bed, wheeled me into the back of a vehicle (supplied by the Motability charity), clamped me in place and strapped me down. Only then did they take me to the chemist's.

The seat belts were suspect, and eventually one snapped. Jim organized repairs, but they could only be done in a workshop in Sherborne, around an hour away. The carers were insistent I had to travel there with them, even though the vehicle was fundamentally unsafe. Fortunately, Jim had a meeting with the NHS at my house that morning, and raised merry hell. The care company begrudgingly gave permission for a three-hour window in which one of their staff could drive the van to and from the garage, but things went from bad to worse. The only way I could go to a restaurant was to book a separate table for the nurses, and pay for their food. Without Jim's financial support, I would have been unable to do so.

The protocols were prohibitive and, it seemed to me, profit-driven. If I wanted to meet a mate in the pub, or go to the cinema, I had to give a week's notice and a so-called care manager had to visit the site twenty-four hours beforehand, to make a risk assessment. Special occasions, such as an invitation to meet Paddy in London for a few drinks and a catch-up, were ripe for exploitation.

One of the carers wheeled me into the pub, where Paddy was waiting, and promptly departed, promising to return after he had found a parking space. He didn't turn up, and later claimed he returned to the hotel because there was nowhere to put the vehicle. The fact Paddy had to organize a specially equipped cab for me didn't seem to register.

The reason for the carer's moonlight flit became apparent in the morning, when I was again left to my own devices while he enjoyed breakfast in bed with one of the other nurses. Talk about friends with benefits . . .

The carers went way beyond their natural responsibilities by recording my telephone calls, and taking screengrabs of my private text messages. Trust was so shattered I started to take my mobile phone and iPad into the shower as a precaution against their prying eyes and ears. When confronted, they claimed they needed to be aware of my intentions to protect me from myself.

It went on and on. I discovered they were using my phone to make international calls to friends and family. They accessed my Sky account and began ordering movies for their own consumption. They raided the drinks cabinet on the ground floor of my house. Worst of all, one of the men, a weasel-faced Canadian guy of Asian descent, stole my iPod.

It is probably for the best that the lads never knew his identity. As it was, Jim had understandable difficulty convincing senior officers that the carers' behaviour was so brazen. I had no privacy, no quality of life. The people employed to keep me fit and well, and offer a semblance of normality, were treating me with complete contempt.

When Jim ensured the contract was cancelled, the response of the care agency was revealing. They tried to shift the blame, portraying me as a difficult client because I wanted to go out and have some sort of life. According to them, I was the problem, constantly challenging their protocols; I didn't want to understand the complexity of their role. As for their staff, they delivered an empty promise that the accusations would be investigated. We're still waiting for a response, nearly a decade later. Today, I am assisted by extremely professional, highly qualified staff. Back then, I was being used by a bunch of chancers who were allowed to challenge my humanity.

It's painful to recall, because I felt hopeless, neglected, diminished. As an elite soldier I had a certain stature and the respect of my peers. The skills, qualities and attributes that enabled me to thrive in a highly disciplined, incredibly demanding world spoke for me. As a disabled man, I was being walked over by people who treated me like a piece of shit.

It doesn't take any great insight into human nature to appreciate the impact of such a demeaning situation. I couldn't even stand up and vent my feelings, face to face. My mental decline accelerated sharply, and my inner voice was insistent: 'How dare they walk over me? What sort of life is this? Where do I go from here? Fuck this, I'm out of here.'

I didn't want to be seen as a charity case. I hated being that wounded soldier, confined to a wheelchair. I resented the fact that I needed support. I was mourning the loss of independence. I experienced all manner of conflicting feelings, and even went through a phase of resenting Jim for all he was doing for me. I couldn't place him in a comfortable compartment. He wasn't a family member, a colleague or an employee.

He was simply a friend.

I didn't know the half of it. He was pulling in favours and making the most of his personal network of contacts. He met secretly in a local pub with the director of operations for Help for Heroes to explain my plight. He was making himself unpopular in certain military circles because he was lobbying aggressively on my behalf.

I would have been lost without him, but to my warped way of

thinking, he was highlighting my incapacities. It was almost as if he was a crutch that I wanted to consign to the back of the nearest cupboard. His concern was acute, if well disguised, but his faith in me never wavered. He was following the logic of Royal Marines training: everything had to break before it could be put back together again.

You have to reach rock bottom, because from there the only way is up.

There were fleeting moments of clarity and hope. One, bizarrely, occurred when someone hacked my laptop, so that I needed a new email address as part of the clean-up. I had the germ of an idea for a campaigning company, with a charitable aim, based on the concept of bravery, so I asked the repair guy to register that as my new domain name. It would be almost four years before I put that initiative into operation, but at least the wheels were turning. For now, I was trapped between my training, and the satisfaction I gained from showing the requisite resolve and mental strength, and my reality, as someone struggling with a toxic mixture of outrage, resentment and self-disgust.

PTSD is a catch-all for a variety of ills, and it seemed a sensible conclusion that I was a sufferer. I'm not so sure, because my dilemma was more complex. I was massively frustrated, for instance, by my failure to find alternative accommodation when a proposed move to a specially adapted barn in Yeovil failed to materialize.

Towards the end of 2013, two and a half years after my discharge from hospital, I was ripping myself apart. I was a man of two halves. Part of me had given up; he was snarling secretly about killing himself. The other part was scathing: 'You fucking loser. What on earth? You're not a quitter. You're a fighter. You've always been a fighter.'

Bad Toby had the keys to the castle.

I had slipped back into terrible habits. I was drinking heavily, and ignoring the warnings of better qualified, but more pliable, sets of carers. I overrode their objections, persuaded my mates to wheel me out with them, and took up residency at the Camel Bar, a nightclub that stayed open until 6 a.m. I could not have cared less about my personal safety; when the carers tried to get me home I told them to piss off.

That flirtation with danger reached a predictable crisis point in the middle of another reckless night. I was outside the club, hopelessly drunk and smoking a cigarette – which in itself was an insane act of self-harm – when the battery servicing my ventilator ran out. It started beeping madly as pandemonium broke out all around me. I should have died but, once again, it wasn't my time. I was saved by the foresight of the club staff, who had an Ambu bag, a resuscitator designed for manual ventilation. One of my mates, acting with the coolness under pressure that defines an elite operative, retrieved it in little more than a minute, fixed on a mask, and began pumping air into my lungs. My carer, meanwhile, hared back to my house to pick up a spare ventilator battery.

I should have been begging for forgiveness and expressing endless gratitude when order was restored, but I was completely nonchalant. I couldn't have cared less if I lived or died. I was off my face, pouring poison into my system. I was just trying to numb the pain, dull the senses. When I eventually sobered up, I realized I couldn't deal with the emotional upset any longer.

I wasn't ready to trust fate. I wanted to decide my destiny. That meant exploring the opportunity for assisted suicide. It's obviously a hugely controversial, acutely personal issue which splits the medical profession, religious philosophers and the general public, but it felt right for me. I regarded being in control of my life, specifically if or how I ended it, as a basic human right.

I began by speaking to my GP about the parameters of the process, and then took legal advice. Though it is illegal in England and Wales, under the Suicide Act of 1961, to assist or encourage another person to take their own life, a patient can make his or her own decisions about receiving or refusing medical treatment under the Mental Capacity Act of 2005.

Two psychologists testified that I was compos mentis, and capable of making my own decisions. I was free to follow a fundamental principle of medical law that, as a patient of sound mind, I had the right to withdraw from treatment, for whatever reason. In my case, that meant inducing death by the act of switching off my ventilator, or removing my tracheostomy tube. I was physically incapable of doing so, but I was advised anyone who did would be protected from prosecution because I would effectively die as a result of my injuries – in other words, of natural causes. I could be eased out as humanely as possible, pain free, by being given opiates like propranolol and morphine beforehand. I know this sounds cold and calculating, but it would be smooth, and slow.

All the paperwork was complete. I had put my financial affairs in order. So why, then, did I draw back from the brink? Where did I find the inner strength to endure? Believe me, it wasn't an act of heroism. I was driven by desperation, and a long overdue acceptance of weakness, to put an end to the slanging match inside my head.

Midway through another seemingly endless night, I had a mental breakdown. I began sobbing and screaming for help in the darkness, and was impossible to console. Everything had piled on top of me. I was scared, and unable to cope. I couldn't manage the crisis on my own. I had been having sessions with a psychiatric nurse on camp, but realized I needed more specialized help.

I poured my heart out to Spot, my military welfare officer, the next morning. I was honest with myself, as much as with him. I was messed up. I couldn't continue to listen to the inner voices condemning me as a coward, or an inadequate. I felt as if I was losing my mind. I was a broken man, completely destroyed, begging for it all to end.

I was conditioned to looking after myself, fixing my problems without assistance. In that world, seeking professional help is easily distorted as an act of craven weakness. I was twenty-eight, but immature for my age. I could no longer sustain my idiocy. My family, my team, came through for me in my hour of need. They steadied me, surrounded me, and found me a refuge.

All I needed was the strength to walk out of the darkness, towards the light.

THIRTEEN

Captain of My Soul

I'VE NEVER BEEN one to hide from the truth. I couldn't come to terms with the man I had become. I was overwhelmed by loneliness and loss. I was at my lowest ebb and couldn't see a purpose in my existence. I didn't know what I was doing in life, so it was best to end it, on my terms. It would be the final gesture of individuality, fortitude and defiance.

Ross Hoar, the psychotherapist for whom I was dredging my soul, and pouring out my heart, listened calmly. A lean, serene man, he was professionally non-committal and gave me space to be myself. Over the eight years we have worked together, since that morning in the psychiatric unit at the Priory Hospital in Southampton, our relationship has become life-affirming.

My trust in him is complete, and our respect is mutual, but it was perhaps as well I didn't know what was going on behind those eyes, looking intently out through black-framed glasses. Ross immediately recognized the strength of my mind, and the seriousness of my intent. His first thought was that if I weren't physically disabled I would have found 'a million ways' to kill myself.

So why, then, did I decide to endure? Over three months in the hospital, a secluded Grade II listed building set in 1.5 acres of the

New Forest, Ross guided me gently towards a T junction. The options were stark: take the left fork and surrender to hopelessness, or turn right and embrace opportunity, in whatever form it takes.

I needed moral support and medication to clear the backlog in my brain. When I was admitted I wasn't eating, and barely communicating. I had told my closest friends and family that I did not want to see them any more. I wasn't taking any phone calls, and didn't check emails.

Cutting myself off was a recipe for disaster because it left me alone with my demons. I was in a dark, scary place, and they were ready to eat me alive. I was grieving, obsessing, and spent countless hours in silent contemplation. I would be wheeled into the grounds or into a conservatory and simply sit there, staring into space.

My room, which offered hints of the depression, anxiety and inner turmoil the unit was set up to deal with, might as well have been a prison cell. It was small, barely big enough for a bed and a chair, with a square window, made of specially strengthened Perspex, set in the door. That window was a haunting symbol of my new reality; every now and again I noticed nurses on suicide watch looking in, to check my well-being. Some patients self-harmed; others were prone to violent episodes.

My life had splintered. It could only be put back together painstakingly, piece by piece. I had to answer the biggest question of all: what made me, me? I couldn't afford a glib answer. During our daily one-hour sessions, Ross recognized I was locked down, mentally. He was at a disadvantage because, contrary to most of his consultations, he couldn't read my body language. My inability to move prevented him from interpreting tell-tale tics and giveaway gestures. Yet, on some deeper level, we connected in a way that I had found impossible with his predecessor, who had a single session with me. He was well regarded in his profession, but I simply could not relate to him on a human level.

Ross made the breakthrough by asking me to outline my three fundamental values, positive qualities that defined me. I chose passion, determination and respect. They were my building blocks. Those traits would give me the dignity I yearned for, the spark I sought and proof of the character I had shown in times of crisis. They also opened up a separate internal debate.

'Who are you? What are you made of? Why is this happening to you? Is it to test your nerve? Do you have the bottle to get through this? How much grit do you have? Are you as real as they say you are? So you think you're made of the strong stuff, do you? Let's find out, shall we?'

It was almost as if I was goading myself into action. I didn't know, deep down, if I was capable of withstanding such searching self-examination, but at least I was willing to try. If I was a disappointment to myself, so be it. I would be able to leave this life with a sense of certainty and completion, with my head held high.

I had reached a turning point. I had made my choice. I was going to give life a damned good go. It was all or nothing. I wasn't going to hesitate, turn back, or stumble. If that happened I would be back at square one, lost and alone. I couldn't handle that. It was the first time since my paralysis that I felt that I still had something to give.

I had been dead to the world. The lights were on, but there was no one at home. By asking me to reaffirm my core values, Ross made me realize what I had retained after my injury. That was a whole lot healthier than dwelling on what that bullet had taken from me. I came to appreciate that, although I was physically a different specimen, I was still the same person inside.

That change in my consciousness changed my life. It was like a piercing ray of sunshine. I've never forgotten that moment of revelation, and pray that I never will. It marked the point when I stood my ground, and raised my eyes to a distant horizon.

Ross didn't have a military background, but his insight was instructive. He told me I wasn't like others he had seen, in a similar state of mind. I wasn't passive. I didn't use the psychiatric unit as a refuge because I was exhausted, and needed to rest before resetting. He sensed an energy within me that was very strong and incredibly destructive.

He felt, correctly, that I had consciously decided I'd had enough. I couldn't see a way forward, and knew what needed to be done. No one was going to stand in my way. His challenge was to channel that certainty in a positive direction, rather than a negative one. It was difficult, because once a guy with my background has set their mind to do something it is very hard to distract or divert them.

He knew he couldn't use a formulaic approach to my condition, because I was so strong-willed I would have simply told him to shove it. I had some prior experience of cognitive behavioural therapy, which is designed to help re-programme the brain, and had found it helpful in understanding and controlling chronic pain.

His message was carefully constructed and cleverly delivered. I was physically disabled, emotionally empty, but in terms of intrinsically who I was – my character, my mind, my focus, my determination, my life force – I was completely intact. We had to work with that, nurture body and soul, for me to step back from the brink.

I knew I was not some sort of nutjob. I just had to reconnect with my spirit.

It was my job to teach Ross the ways of my world, the culture that underpins the Royal Marines and Special Forces. I used, as an example, how for several years I had spent hours, each morning, attempting to move a finger. I told myself that shouldn't be beyond a decent Marine, and I intended to live up to the green beret by continuing to try.

The best way to get a Marine to do something is to tell him he can't manage it.

Ross got it. We spoke about how to get that bloody-mindedness working for me, rather than against me. That wouldn't be easy, since I had to face the brutal reality that I would remain paralysed. I had still to deal with inevitable irritations and inconveniences. He found the key by challenging me to dictate my own destiny, and decide what success would look like.

That appealed to an ingrained sense of self-reliance, and involved a negotiation with myself. Sure, I could distract myself, keep myself busy, but I had to confront the fact there was no way around certain limitations. I switched focus, to the benefits of my mental strength and the power of my personality. I didn't shy away from my problems, as many people would.

I don't play tricks with the truth. Fulfilment, for me, involves allowing others to share the lessons of my failures and frustrations. It also involves imparting the knowledge I've gained along the way, without boasting about my achievements. I've seen what works for me. I've come to an understanding of how I can get as much out of life as possible.

In its simplest terms, that is the aim for everybody, isn't it? This is what I can do. This is what I can't do. This is what I am. This is what I want from life. This is how I am going to get it.

This book is part of the process of realignment. It took me a decade to decide to write it. I probably would not have done so but for the number of guys within the Special Forces who encouraged me to bring my story to a wider audience. They knew, as well as I did, it would take me down some pretty dark alleys. Their respect was unspoken, but meaningful beyond measure.

I don't need a TikTok video or a social media following to feed my ego, but if I can influence one person to look beyond the restrictions of their life, my presence on the planet will have been worthwhile. I hope this doesn't sound trite, but I'd implore you to see the person, not the wheelchair, because, given the chance, they will give of themselves to you.

Body image is important. I still find it very hard to deal with the fact most people don't see me, though they stare at me. Their focus is on the disability, the chair, and the tubes coming out of my throat. It's not the staring that bothers me, though it can be off-putting, but the fact they have no idea who I am, what I've done, where I've been, what I've seen.

Going out into society is difficult, because it is hard to convey my humanity to strangers. My identity has been transformed, from a very physical, supremely fit individual who projected an aura of quiet confidence and steely determination. I know the characteristics of my inner self are largely unchanged but there are still days when I tell myself, 'For God's sake, there's no way I am still me.'

There's a paradox in play. When people understand the complexity and complications of my journey, they tend to be genuinely impressed. When they tell me I must be proud of what I have achieved they do so in the spirit of it being the biggest compliment they can pay me. I hate it because it sounds like complete bullshit.

That's a reflection on me, rather than them. It took me some time to figure out why I react in that manner, but I reached the conclusion that praise comes over to me as patronizing, even when it is innocent and not intended to be so. That's one of my biggest flaws.

Ross believes it is a legacy of my injury. I still carry a judgement, a deeply buried resentment that I didn't deserve what happened to me. He has worked with me on reading other people, to identify their good intentions. I have to accept there are certain individuals who feel sorry for me, and don't know how to connect. That usually means they are super awkward or incredibly polite around me.

Once he had pointed that out, I began to notice behaviour patterns. We would be sat together, talking in the grounds of the Priory during that long hot summer of 2014; staff members would ignore Ross and say hello to me in a sing-song sort of voice. They were trying too hard to be nice, if that makes sense. It made me sullen, and unwilling to open up conversations.

That conflict surfaced whenever I was asked how I was. I wanted to shut out the small talk and, at best, would mumble that old white lie – 'I'm fine' – before making it clear I wasn't in the mood for idle chatter. Ross, inevitably, picked up on that.

'You do know what "fine" stands for, don't you?' he asked, deadpan. 'Fucked up, insecure, neurotic and emotional.'

Point taken.

As time went by, I began to acquire perspective by projecting my problems through the prism of other patients. Their problems were raw, real, and relatable. One of them insisted he had been paralysed for ten years before being miraculously healed. Complete nonsense, of course, but he spoke with utter certainty about the experience. He asked me about my condition, and tried to comfort me by assuring me he related to my ordeal.

It turned out he suffered from schizophrenia, and switched between four or five different personalities. Another of his characters was born to alien parents after being abducted to their home planet. He had returned to Earth to study human behaviour, and was following his mother's instructions to watch every alien movie, since there was a hidden message in each one. He was way out there, lost in himself, watching films like *Independence Day* obsessively and trying, whenever possible, to convince us the movies were fact, not fiction. Bless him. He was a really nice guy, leaping from identity to identity. He couldn't dress himself, and often became confused, but he was completely harmless.

Other inmates were a danger to themselves, and those around them. I never discovered his precise psychological disorder, but one poor soul would run naked through the corridors, screaming, and had continually to be restrained. He took great interest in our art group and was found, in the dead of one particular night, in the small art room, eating tubes of our paint.

Several individuals in the unit suffered from more conventional eating disorders. They radiated sadness. I met one lovely lady, who could not have been much older than eighteen, and tried to offer what solace I could. She was timid, as quiet as a mouse, and terrified of food. It wasn't just a resistance to taste or texture, it was a full-blown phobia. She was on a drip, in a wheelchair, unable to walk because her anorexia had made her so weak. I made a point of trying to accompany her at mealtimes and, ironically given my previous reluctance to engage, get her to concentrate on inconsequential chatter. The problem was that if she had more than three or four peas on her plate, she would shake uncontrollably and succumb to a panic attack.

Once she calmed down we would sit together in the grounds. I ignored her illness, and talked to her randomly to try and give her some respite from her plight. I would ramble on about my experiences, tell her stories from my childhood, ask about her family, and where she came from. She had so little energy she could barely speak, hardly string a sentence together.

It's such a cruel condition. I don't know whether she recovered, but I pray that she found peace.

We could hear the screams from the children's ward, on the floor below. The kids were kept separate from us, for obvious reasons, but they seemed to be causing chaos. We'd pick up second-hand stories of teenagers self-harming, of social misfits causing trouble and trying to run away. We'd often see search parties being sent out from the grounds to bring them back again.

The place had a weird sense of community. Though the addiction unit was another which operated in isolation, it is difficult to avoid one another. I came across quite a few recovering alcoholics, going through their initial thirty-one-day detox, and recognized the signs of self-analysis – a reliable indication of intensive therapy.

The Priory allowed me to appreciate the range of life as it can be. There are a lot of people out there, suffering in different ways for different reasons, but we are all equally relevant as human beings. That's very special, when you come to think of it. We each have our own traumas, and our individual tipping points. Mine came with the realization I was not an island.

When I was admitted to the hospital I had never been more vulnerable. My anxiety levels were through the roof because people could easily take advantage of me. I didn't see a solution, because I had been through a horrendous period in which I was at the mercy of unreliable individuals. The level of risk in my life was off the scale.

Once I was confident in the consistency and continuity of the care team around me I made a huge step forward. It gave me a greater sense of control, and a new mindset. I still have my dark moments, when the pain gnaws away at me, but I know that all things being equal, today will be manageable, so I can focus on what else I can build into my life.

I'm still wary. My radar still has a high frequency. I don't want to get burned again. But I've come a long way from the point at which I was being sucked into a death spiral. There's work to do in this area, but I'm coming to terms with the fact that people want to help me out of the goodness of their heart, rather than an underlying sense of pity.

It's been a process of acceptance without dousing my inner fire. I've rationalized that I arouse different instincts in people. Some want to mother me. Others want to protect me, shelter me. That's an unintentional but direct challenge to my self-esteem, and my male pride. I don't want to be mollycoddled. My instinct has always been to take risks, to push on.

One of the great attractions of serving in the Special Forces is the autonomy you are given. I was the captain of my soul. I made my own choices, even if they sometimes exceeded my capabilities. That freedom has gone. My life changed, instantly, without warning or preparation. Ross likened it to taking a sucker punch to the face: there's no time to back away, cover up, or minimize the punishment.

I'm still evaluating the damage, but my resentment at my fate is positive, since without that I could easily succumb to complacency and indifference. To give a recent example, I was livid because the internal lift in my house had broken down, stranding me upstairs. It reinforced my powerlessness and made me difficult to live with. I saw the glances of the care team: 'Ooh, Toby's angry.' So? What are we saying here, that I have to be happy every day? Can't I have an off day, when I give vent to my feelings? That's being alive, isn't it?

Never will I die.

Live for the day. Keep going.

Link the past with the present, and the future.

Think of life as a yomp across the Brecon Beacons. The terrain is testing. There are peaks and troughs. There are dangers and distractions. What are you going to do? Feel sorry for yourself? Give up, and crawl into a ditch? No. You are going to keep putting one foot in front of the other. You are going to drive yourself forward towards the next checkpoint, however distant that seems.

Ross once quoted the slogan on a fridge magnet to me: 'Courage doesn't scream and shout. It just says that in the morning I am going to try again.' I don't tend to pay any attention to motivational mottos, but that one certainly struck a chord. I'm living that catchphrase, day by day. I've got the same drive to live as I once had to die.

We talk about death a lot. I live with its reality. It could come without warning, like my injury, but Ross has given me its context. He remembers the colour draining from my face as we sat in a pub car park in Lyndhurst, of all places, talking about the nature of mortality. It was a surreal but personally significant conversation.

'Toby, you do realize that most people die quietly, with people around them, in care homes or in their own bed? Your whole frame of reference is distorted because only a relatively small percentage of people will die suddenly and violently.'

'What? Surely that's not true . . .'

He had completely blown my mind. The thought that people could die happily and peacefully, just sort of falling asleep, was completely alien to my experience. I'd seen men go out kicking and screaming, in the blood and gore of a battlefield. That death involving extreme pain and suffering was far from the norm was a revelation to me. Something shifted, deep inside. It gave me a degree of peace.

Maybe I am not going to die horribly, in a traumatic, frightening way. I've come close to death, confronted it. I've felt its cold shudder. I respect that some people do not want to face the prospect, but I think it is important to talk about death, freely and openly, because of its inevitability.

I'm not going to underplay suffering, because I've yet to fully get over the passing of my stepdad in 2018. He was taken painfully, by cirrhosis of the liver. It was very sudden, and I never got to say goodbye, because I could not get back to South Africa, through no fault of my own. I hate my injury for preventing me from attending his funeral and paying proper respect.

Ross tells me his job is to accompany me, in a philosophical sense, wherever I want to go. I wouldn't say he is the reason I am still here, but he is a reminder of why I am here. Without him being around, to pick me up in moments of dire need, I'd be in an entirely different situation. I'm not afraid to admit I've occasionally strayed from our ideals: I'm human and I fall down, now and again.

I now have to respond to a series of absolutes: take this medication, undertake this manipulation, and be aware of that potential complication. To a degree that is true of anyone with a chronic illness, but my individualism means a lot to me. I still recite the mantra of my three core values: passion, determination and respect.

I'm not sure I convinced everyone that I was ready to leave the Priory, but my honesty was in my favour. I told them that I felt a lot better, and was ready to face the world again. I knew there would be bumps in the road, and times when my compass would go haywire, but I was in a healthy enough condition to deserve their trust.

I had reached that T junction, thanks to the subtle steering of my psychotherapist, and taken the right fork, towards opportunity. I had completed the process of parting from the person who, in a sense, had died in the darkness in Afghanistan. I had decided to make something of my life, and had a lot to give.

I made a promise to myself: if I was going to go for it, I was really going to go for it.

FOURTEEN

Beautiful Minds

ONCE I DECIDED to stop existing, and start living, my world expanded.

On the balance of probability, I had proved the doctors wrong by surviving. I had come to terms with my limitations, and was determined not to be defined by them. I needed to stop dwelling on what I could not do, and concentrate on what I could do. Freedom, I discovered in my darkest time, in that psychiatric unit, is a state of mind.

There wasn't a eureka moment, when depression lifted, the clouds parted, and my days were filled with sweetness and light. There were still moments of despair, when I wondered whether it was all worth it, but, gradually, I felt a strange sense of serenity. I had a purpose, a plan, and an identifiable future on which to focus.

I might have been imprisoned by my body, but my brain allowed me out on parole.

Formal education offered a level playing field, a re-entry point into society. An examination paper doesn't differentiate. It is a gauge of ability rather than disability. I didn't want any favours; I've never sought sympathy or special treatment. I would be judged on my own merits. I wanted my humanity back.

I had to start from scratch, which, to be honest, was a bit of a blow.

It wasn't going to be quite the breeze I envisaged. I had somehow matriculated from high school in South Africa at eighteen, having done the equivalent of my A levels, but my qualifications were irrelevant. I started the process of re-education on camp, with Jim Patrick as my tutor. Jim had been a maths teacher before he joined the navy.

It was a healing process. I was no longer weighed down by the apparent futility of the struggle, the medical minutiae and grinding worry. I had a new view on life. I appreciated how precious it was, despite its imperfections and indignities. I needed to make every moment count. If I was going to do something it was not enough merely to do it well. I had to excel.

That meant employing a military mindset. I reasoned that my ultimate ambition of running my own company was dependent on reaching a series of checkpoints. Jim would break down the subject in what was essentially a series of briefings, illustrated by examples on a whiteboard. I would memorize his points as best I could. The brain is, after all, a muscle. My progress depended on redeveloping muscle memory.

Everyone told me it would take six months, at least, to pass what is a minimum one-year course. I did it in three months, with an A* grade. So much for the doctors who suggested I would struggle to retain information if I didn't get sufficient rest. (Maybe those informal maths lessons I gave the lads between operations in Afghan weren't in vain . . .) All I needed, when I periodically fell asleep during lessons, was the energy boost of a chocolate bar, fed to me by Jim. He understood my perfectionism. If, when we did a test, I got only thirteen out of fifteen, I insisted on returning to it until I answered every question correctly.

My next checkpoint involved passing A levels in Business Studies, Law, English Literature and Philosophy at Bournemouth & Poole College. This was another leap of faith, the first time I had mixed constantly with strangers. I felt like little Johnny on his first day at primary school, albeit without the new satchel, shiny shoes and blazer with growing room. I arrived in a bulky electronic wheel-chair, with an intensive care nurse and a care assistant, to be greeted by Gill Akhurst, who had volunteered to be my guide.

Gill calmed my initial fear, that no one would be able to under-stand me due to the mechanical wheezing of my ventilator. She offered to abandon my online induction test when it asked whether I liked dancing, and what hand I wrote with. I decided to ignore the absurdity of the situation, make up the answers, and press on to the Spaghetti Challenge.

That involved joining a group of four understandably awkward students, and sitting there like a lemon as they made a tower out of raw pasta and marshmallows. Out of the corner of my eye I could see people staring at me, and knew I needed to balance self-belief with an awareness of my difficulties. Anything less and I would just crum-ble with shyness and embarrassment.

If it was daunting for me, it was one helluva culture shock for my classmates. Half of them looked at the tube in my throat and won-dered if I'd be able to breathe properly, let alone talk. Most of them had never interacted socially with anyone in a wheelchair. I was thirty; they were school leavers, aged between sixteen and eighteen. No wonder they were stand-offish. They simply didn't know how to approach me. Some said hello and backed away instinctively, as if I was going to bite them. I wasn't offended. I was so far outside the realms of their experience. Besides, I had other things to worry about, like negotiating crowded corridors. Reaching the classroom was an obstacle course of narrow doorways and deceptive inclines.

Really young kids, and elderly people, tend to be direct: 'What's the matter with you, then?' Brits are, in general, reserved. The barriers go up in adolescence. I could hear the whispers between my new classmates, daring one another to talk to me. They were clearly conflicted between curiosity and discomfort.

Early on, they preferred to deal in rumours, rather than reality. I picked up the buzz that I was a rugby player, found broken at the bottom of a scrum. Understandable, I suppose, but I didn't get a chance to address it until lessons began in earnest, and we operated in groups. You speak to one person, who speaks to their mates, who pass on the message to others until everyone understands.

Yeah. I was shot in the neck. I shouldn't be alive. But since I am, I'm going to make the most of it.

We were good for one another. As they relaxed in my company, they lost their self-consciousness and went beyond obvious questions about what had happened to me. Of course they wanted to hear the war stories in all their gory detail, but we discussed everything from the cruelty of fate and political morality to the thrill of surfing a big wave and the madness of motocross.

I was their unofficial tutor in the ways of the world. They lapped up my life lessons, and helped me more than they knew. I had forgotten the simple pleasure of basic human interaction, shared laughter and affinity with a group of individuals united by circumstance. It is easy to become savagely lonely and self-centred in isolation.

I realized how much I had missed the idealism and energy of

youth. They were brilliant students, so bubbly and blissfully unaware of how hard life can be. They were naive, but that isn't meant as a criticism. It was beautiful. If I empowered and intrigued them with my stories, they returned the favour by reminding me what it was like to attack life, as opposed to being overwhelmed by it.

Any negativity was rare, and fleeting. When I first turned up in his class, one lecturer exclaimed to Gill, 'How's he going to learn, then? How is he going to do his work?' Since he was standing next to me at the time, without registering my presence, he received my standard response to such thoughtless ignorance.

'"He" has a name. Talk to me, not about me, or even at me. I am not a piece of wood or a pillar of stone. I am not invisible. I have thoughts, feelings and capabilities. I belong, too.'

The message registered. From that moment on, he was consistently supportive.

Another, who kept repeating 'Is he compos mentis, then?' in mock incredulity, was marginalized as a figure of fun. I'm not going to let such ridiculousness get me down. I'm going to try to set a better example. I'll keep doing what I'm doing.

No one is worthless. Life is never meaningless.

The rest of the tutors were great, even if some, bizarrely, seemed a little in awe of me. They'd never had a mature student with my level of disability, but they recognized a pupil who was desperate to study and anxious to achieve. Once they'd picked up on my back story, they understood the intensity of my ambition, and did everything they could to help. I was around the same age as some of them. They felt comfortable dealing with me as an adult. I was almost a halfway house between them and the students.

I have always been pretty chilled as a character away from active service, so I could shoot teenage shit with the best of them without coming across as a tragic old duffer. They made me forget I was paralysed, and got the old juices flowing. Their default position if they didn't understand something in class was silence. Free from the reservations of youth, and unconcerned by the danger of losing face, I didn't mind asking potentially daft questions. I wasn't afraid to challenge the teachers to clarify points, or explain principles.

I could have had my work officially differentiated because of the difficulties. Potential concessions ranged from a reduction in its volume to a free pass from group activity. They even carried the promise of special dispensation in marking. No chance. If the class was doing a five-thousand-word essay I wasn't going to cheat my way through by submitting half that.

If the subject was hard, I wasn't looking for a short cut. If I am going to do something, I'm going to do it properly. That's the way I have always lived my life, straight down the line. No preferential treatment, no undeserved opportunities, no false equivalences. If I couldn't respect myself for taking an easy way out, why should I expect others to respect me?

The practicalities of my care needs were complicated. Then, as now, I needed a 'cough assist' machine linked to the mains, to push more air into my lungs to clear them of secretions, and open up my airways. My stomach still has to be compressed on a daily basis, to keep my blood pressure up and avoid the possibility of fainting.

My breathing patterns are enforced, rather than natural. The ventilator is set at eighteen breaths a minute; I have to time my sentences, otherwise I run out of air before I can complete them. It's now a subconscious process, but I've had to learn to talk as I inhale and exhale. The louder I speak, the more air I require; if I shout, I can barely get a single word out.

Everyday incidents were challenging. I would be startled, at the end of lessons, by the banging of seats being hastily vacated. This isn't a manifestation of PTSD, but loud bangs frighten me when I fail to anticipate them. I can't work out why, but I feel myself getting angry. It fills me with an illogical rage.

In academic terms, Gill was my lifesaver. A retired police officer, she was calm and measured, a cut above the other note takers originally assigned to me. Employed by the college, she was quickly excused other duties so she could work with me full-time. The authorities rapidly turned a blind eye to her breaking house rules by visiting me out of hours, to oversee my homework.

Just handing me her notes at the end of lessons wasn't a great deal of use. I was obviously unable to type or write, and didn't have voice recognition software, because it went haywire when it picked up the ventilator. When I had essays to complete Gill would prop her notes up in my eyeline and take down my dictation without me seeing what she was writing. When I was on my own, revising, I would memorize key phrases. Ours is a special relationship, based on trust.

She was obliged to be completely impartial, and had to deal with the self-imposed pressure of her responsibilities to me. We were engaged in a game of patience, through no fault of our own. I had to learn to articulate my thoughts concisely and accurately. In theory, putting them down on paper should be relatively simple. In practice, it was difficult. Sometimes they came out all wrong.

Compensation came in other areas of coursework. I had half-formed ideas of setting up a business in the extreme sports area, and was eager to research the Red Bull model, as a case study. The company proved to be innovative, inter-dependent, fast-moving and, because of its charitable arm, Wings for Life, personally relevant.

Dietrich Mateschitz, Red Bull's founder, set up the charity in 2003 when Hannes Kinigadner, son of his friend Heinz, the two-time world motocross champion, was left tetraplegic at the age of nineteen after being thrown from his motorcycle during a race in Austria. He survived two cardiac arrests, a cerebellar stroke and the immediate threat of suffocation. Specialists in spinal cord injury from across the world were invited to the company's headquarters in Salzburg. A research foundation was established to investigate the possibility of damaged nerve cells regenerating through new therapies and interventions. Hannes, who unlike me has limited use of his arms, remains paralysed, but at least he has hope.

The Business Studies course also allowed me to assess Elon Musk's commercial philosophies. I felt a natural pride in his achievements, as a fellow South African. At last glance he was worth around $180 billion, and I found the lessons of his creativity, imagination and vision priceless. Fearless, personally and professionally, he has pushed the boundaries all the way into space.

In an entirely different way, Dylan Thomas was also my type of guy. I had been raging against the dying of the light long before I studied him, as the James Dean of poetry. I related to his impulsiveness. Like me, he was a natural outsider. He made sense of my early life, in particular, as a maverick who didn't care about the consequences of refusing to play by the rules.

Elsewhere in English Literature, I struggled with Thomas Hardy's version of Victorian sexual morality, *Tess of the d'Urbervilles*. I couldn't really decipher Shakespeare until I put him into my own context. *Romeo and Juliet* is a classic love story, but his depiction of the family feud between the Montagues and the Capulets, and his understanding of the underlying tribalism, spoke to the soldier in me.

Trust me, the dynamics of the houses of Verona are repeated, with similarly fatal consequences, on a regular basis in Afghanistan.

I injected a little comedy into the tragedy during a readthrough, when I was obliged to be on stage. Gill offered to accompany me to hold my script, which might have made the necessary suspension of disbelief a little difficult. Instead I got her to scribble my lines all over my hands – a decent idea until I realized it wouldn't scrub off in time for an important meeting on camp.

Learning is easier if you relate it to personal experience. At one level, Law is a dry, intimidating subject, but I approached it on a practical basis. What could it teach me about life? How could it help me understand the way the world works? What did it tell me about how and why society was held together? I was intrigued, because there were more questions than answers.

I took a similar approach to Philosophy. These weren't a bunch of dead blokes being clever. They were connected, and relevant. Aristotle taught me the power of persuasion. Plato, his teacher, spoke convincingly about justice, equality, politics and beauty. Socrates, Plato's tutor, emphasized the superiority of the mind over the body and paid for his beliefs by being executed by hemlock poisoning.

They came alive for me through their thoughts and theories, but when I looked around at the rest of the kids in class they were passive. They regurgitated the quotes without enthusiasm or meaning, and were hesitant in joining in the debates. At first I was puzzled, because they were a bright bunch, but then I realized my life experience gave me an advantage.

They thought the subject was complicated. I regarded it as common sense. They took philosophical beliefs as statements of fact, instead of challenging them. I questioned everything. Who were these guys? What credibility did they have? How did they get their messages across? Were they products of their time? I stressed how important it is to look deeply into any given situation.

Don't take things at face value, or leap to conclusions, on the say-so of someone else.

Looking back, that attitude reflected a surge in self-confidence. I was no longer submissive, crushed by the weight of the world. My plans for a new company, Bravery, were coming together. I wanted to do something exceptional and different, something that bucked the trend and was bigger than the sum of its parts. It wasn't just about making money; I was also laying down the foundations of my charity for underprivileged children.

The teenage nutcase earned A* grades in his four A levels. He was off to Bournemouth University, blissfully unaware of how tough it would be.

I was ready for the academic challenge, and the continual complications of my injuries, but nothing could have prepared me for the mortifying experience of being forced to sit in a wheelchair at the front of a lecture hall containing four hundred students, to avoid disruption. I could feel eyes boring into my back, and hear murmurs of alarm and amusement.

I couldn't look around, to confirm my suspicions. I reckon I'm pretty strong-willed, but psychologically, I was all over the place. My mind was playing every horrible trick in the book. I wanted the ground to swallow me up. Had I suddenly become the prize exhibit in a freak show? Was this a step too far? Did I deserve to be there? All I could do was stay true to myself.

Have courage. Stand up for your beliefs. Focus on the end goal. Don't worry about what other people think.

It was daunting, and didn't get any easier. Some of the seminar rooms were unfit for purpose. The doors were barely broad enough to allow my chair access. Group sessions involved classmates moving their desks around, to let me and Gill sit among them, like a pair of sore thumbs. My nurse and carer were pushed to the margins.

It wasn't the fault of the students, another collection of beautiful minds. They quickly identified with my story, but I struggled. For the first time in a long time, quitting seemed a simple, sensible option. I would listen to that sneering voice in my head, telling me I wasn't worthy, and come up with all sorts of excuses not to attend lectures.

I'm not feeling too well today. The car could do with a service. The traffic is so bad I'd be late anyway. They won't miss me.

My days would begin at 4 a.m. with three hours of personal care, which ranged from manipulative exercises to being washed, dressed and having my teeth cleaned. It was a long, exhaustive process, and I would often be shattered by the start of lectures at 9 a.m. Whenever I nodded off, which was obvious since I'm hardly a silent sleeper, Gill would drop something to regain my attention. I'd whisper something like 'Did you get everything, Gill?' and she would threaten to pinch my ear if I took another nap. We needed to keep it light-hearted, because logistics were difficult. The final class of the day began at 7 p.m. That coincided with shift changes for my carers, so it required up to six trips to get everyone in the right position.

The financial elements of my university examinations, especially profit and loss accounts, were a nightmare. I had to tell Gill what numbers to punch into my calculator and instruct her to place the answers in a specific column. Gill had to register my answer, even if she knew it was wrong. I had to double- and treble-check my calculations to avoid a mistake, since there was no margin for error.

When an obvious inaccuracy crept in it short-circuited the whole process. I had to go through my workings yet again, trying to figure out what I'd done wrong. Gill was concerned that any discrepancy was down to her. I allowed myself a single drink of water in the six hours it took to complete the Finance exam. No wonder she was a nervous wreck and I was physically shattered and in need of manipulation at the end of it.

I would often go into spasm, because of changes in temperature, but the integral challenge was more mental than physical. I habitually over-compensate for my injury, and feel a need to prove myself, but that was balanced by the buzz I got from group work at university. Students respected me as a natural organizer: I got things done.

In return, I recognized their humanity. Maybe I wasn't the social outcast I thought I was.

There were other stumbling blocks, most notably a tutor who tended to mark me down after making it clear she objected to my military background, yet I kept with the programme, and did what I set out to do. I'm particularly proud of the associated research project I completed, into the sustainability of water provision in Third World countries.

The moment I learned I had earned a first-class degree in Business is imprinted on my brain. It was phenomenal. I wasn't emotional because of the outcome, but because of how far I had travelled, spiritually, to get there. I could still achieve. I still had something to give. I am an obsessive. No matter how tough it gets, I will try harder.

I still couldn't bring myself to attend the graduation ceremony, though. Some SF attitudes to public recognition die hard. Gill collected my degree diploma for me, and returned with the news that I had picked up the year's outstanding achievement award, voted on by every lecturer in the faculty. I guess I should have paused and reflected on what that meant, but I couldn't.

I also couldn't control the wider reaction. My friends and former colleagues in the services were blown away. Strangers were dumbfounded. A theme emerged: people couldn't work out how someone in my condition had managed it. When I explained my hopes and fears, the highs and lows and the whys and wherefores, I was struck by how they questioned themselves.

Wow, they reasoned. If this guy can do this, what's my excuse for not pushing myself?

It dawned on me that perhaps I had a tale to tell, beyond the usual breathless recitation of battlefield incident. I'm not the type to blow smoke up my own backside (in my condition that's physically impossible anyway), but I was struck by how many people felt I had a wider vocation, in teaching through example.

I've been told I instil something in people that makes them want to better themselves. Another lad at uni, paralysed but with greater motor control, cited me as his inspiration in pursuing his degree. That's pretty humbling, and it makes me confirm my own choices in pushing myself. When you've been as close to taking your own life as I have, that can be a painful process. I'm far from perfect, but I've found a sense of perspective.

For me, life has meaning not in self-worth, or material benefits, but in what I can do to help other people become better individuals. Seeing someone achieve because of something I've said or done is its own reward. I hope I'm not getting too pious or philosophical here, but we live in a world that is divided, very harsh, and getting worse.

Despite that, I refuse to believe human beings are instinctively programmed to do bad things. I've always believed people innately know what is right and wrong. Sometimes, of course, life can distort. It can mess with the head. It is easy to stall. I've seen some terrible things, but have never lost my faith in my fellow man.

I know this is a cliché, but over the years I have learned to value life in all its forms. I'm trying to be more understanding, in seeing things through the eyes of other people. Just as they cannot be expected to appreciate how difficult things can be for me, I need to do better in grasping the reasons why they act as they do.

People ask me all the time where I want to get to, and what I want ultimately to achieve. I struggle to answer, since when I get there I know I'll move on, and simply set new goals. I've never been satisfied. I've never reached the point where I've said to myself, 'That's it. I can die a happy man now.'

There's too much to live for.

FIFTEEN

Bravery

THE WORD 'BRAVERY' captures the imagination. It conjures images of firemen running into blazing buildings, lifeboat crews launching into raging seas, policemen confronting armed criminals, and soldiers putting their lives on the line for their comrades. I've seen that type of courage, but bravery is so much more than that. It is an overarching virtue that comes in all shapes and forms.

I believe bravery underpins basic human qualities which are so easily overlooked in today's crazy, fractured world. You have to be brave to be honest, fair or unselfish. You have to be brave to stand up for what you believe in, to show compassion and, occasionally, contrition. You have to be brave to set your sights high, beyond what you are told is possible.

You also have to possess a private form of bravery, to face your own truths.

For me, that involves waking up every day knowing the situation I am in, and not falling into despair. Every morning is just as hard as the last four and a half thousand or so mornings I've endured since I was paralysed. It doesn't get any easier confronting my problems, however familiar they become. They're inescapable.

My capacity to cope says more about me than my mention in

despatches for gallantry in Afghanistan. I'm not disparaging the honour of such recognition, which is a source of great pride to me, but it reflects conventional courage in the form of guys consciously putting themselves in harm's way when the bullets are flying and the senses are scrambled by explosions.

I've witnessed incredible acts of valour. The temptation is to hide, to take cover, to bug out (to use a soldier's slang), but people have stayed in the line of fire to fight for their fellow man. They knew full well they could die at any second. There's no romanticism involved. When you get shot, you just get turned off. The finality is terrifying.

I've seen friends make the ultimate sacrifice, and give their life for the cause, for their mates. I'm visualizing their faces as I read these words, hearing their laughter, and feeling their presence. They were taking it to the insurgents, head-on. As time moves on, I'm increasingly reluctant to refer to our adversaries as the enemy, because that makes them out to be intrinsically different from us.

We all bleed. We are merely separated by variations in cultures and beliefs.

I'm still here because of that sort of bravery, which almost becomes routine when so many of the wounded are extracted from the battlefield under massive fire. People instinctively run in to save their mates in the middle of a firefight, as they did for me. They thought of nothing other than getting me out of there, though my situation seemed hopeless. They saved my life.

I've also seen the opposite of that, the cowardliness and cruelty involved in using women and children as human shields. I've seen Taliban commanders scuttle away in an attempt to save themselves, leaving their families and their men to their fate. What sort of human being does that? As terrible as it is to contemplate, they walk among us.

That's the worst form of human nature. The moral courage required to look beyond your fears and suspicions, and help your fellow man, identifies the best elements of our species. To me, those ideals were exemplified by our medics, who had to balance their professional instincts to tend the stricken with the sombre realities of a combat situation.

Put yourself in their position for a moment. You are tired, stressed, coming towards the end of a seemingly endless shift during which your operating base has been under persistent rocket attack. You hear shouts from the edge of the compound, register the alarm in the voices, and naturally move towards the scene of the commotion.

An injured civilian has arrived, carrying what seems to be the lifeless form of a child. As a medic, confronted by someone pleading for help, you are trained to offer what support you can. As a human being, you imagine the poor man's anguish. As a soldier, you sense a potential trap. It is not beyond the bounds of possibility that the civilian is a suicide bomber. As awful as this appears, the boy's body could be a prop.

The safest option is to turn them away. If you offer assistance, tend the man's wounds and search for signs of life in the child, you may be storing up trouble for the future. One, or even both, may eventually recover. They could return, armed and with deadly intent, and kill you and your brothers. They could be waiting behind mud walls, ready to ambush your patrols.

Without exception, our medics faced their fears and did their human duty. They tried to save lives. All lives. We don't live in a perfect world, however. Other soldiers failed to reach their standards of behaviour, and occasionally let themselves down in the heat of the moment, because they were consumed by anger and a misplaced sense of power.

In war, a soldier's mind can become a little warped. Again, put yourself in his position. You've been sleeping on the floor for weeks. You've seen your mates get hurt. An ache in your gut, and sourness in the throat, testifies to a combination of constant tension and grinding dirt. You're on edge, and want to take it out on someone.

You set out to humiliate the locals, punish them for crimes they did not commit. You want to ruin their houses, trample on their crops. You intend to take out your frustrations on their livestock, destroy their few precious belongings, like pots and pans and tin tea sets. Just for the sake of it. Just because you think you can.

I'm not saying I am some sort of saint, and I understand the thought processes involved, however damaging and mistaken they may be. But you have to rise above such base behaviour. You have to be better than that. I won't lie: the temptations are powerful and obvious. Actively resisting them, or preventing them being enacted, is fraught with difficulty.

One incident stands out in memory. I remember it so clearly. A senior officer, who outranked me, was screaming and shouting, stomping on vegetables being grown in a small plot inside a compound. The locals were visibly frightened, cowering. This man, my superior, was in the process of literally taking food out of their mouths.

I was compelled to react to what I saw as an indefensible abuse of power. 'What the fuck are you doing?' I yelled. 'That's wrong, bang out of order. Don't forget why you are here, man. Take your head for a shit.'

As you can imagine, the challenge to authority did not go down well. He came for me, and we stared each other out, face to face.

I had gone too far to back down. I warned him: 'Do that again, and you'll see what happens.'

In military terms, such insolence usually brings consequences, but though we were wary of each other for some time, at some deeper level he must have realized he was in the wrong. Nothing more was said of it; the clash was chalked up to experience.

I'm often told that I am brave for persevering with injury and illness. It's well intentioned, but a brittle sort of praise, because I don't recognize the heroic figure that some make me out to be. It flies in the face of everything I believe about myself. I'm nothing special. I'm not particularly brave. I'm just trying to do what I've got to do to get by.

There's no shame in being scared. It's a natural reaction. In the words of my hero, Nelson Mandela, when he looked back on his time in prison on Robben Island, 'I learned that courage was not the absence of fear, but the triumph over it. The brave man is not he who does not feel afraid, but he who conquers that fear.'

I'd acknowledged my fear after returning from my first tour of Afghanistan with the Royal Marines, and felt it again going out for my second tour, with the Special Forces. I knew full well the odds on me surviving had shifted. I was playing the lottery with my life again. Fate did what fate does.

I was terribly afraid when I returned to married quarters at the base, after being discharged from the Priory. I knew I was returning to an unbearable situation. I feared being stuck there for the foreseeable future. I dreaded being forgotten, discarded. I knew if that happened, I would fall back into old habits. I would become increasingly depressed, and impatient to die.

It took eleven months, and a humbling amount of help from so many good people, before I was able to move out and into my current, specially adapted house. In that time I discovered the power of hope. My life lesson is best summed up by a quote from another of South Africa's greatest role models, Archbishop Desmond Tutu: 'Hope is being able to see that there is light, despite all of the darkness.'

I maintained my inner belief, that I was put on this planet for a reason. I hope that doesn't come across as arrogant, overblown or even flippant; it's my clumsy way of saying that I want to make a difference, however I do so and whatever that might be. I'm just following my instincts, because there is a lot of good in the world that is worth fighting for.

I've done some daft things, especially as a kid, but in the main I have tried to do the right things for the right reasons. As I've mentioned, my military training merely reinforced my conviction that if I am going to do something, I will go the extra mile to ensure it is done properly. I want my life to have a purpose, and the correct moral underpinning.

That's why I named my business, the symbol of my recovery, Bravery. The ethos and message of the company sits so well with what that word represents. It is the core which runs through it.

I want it to make a difference, and consciously challenge the normal way of commerce, which is fundamentally profit-driven. I'm determined never to listen to the accountant, standing over my shoulder and wondering, pointedly, about the health of the number on the bottom line.

I need to eat, as much as the next man. Principles don't fill anyone's plate. I understand making a profit is one of the core functions of any business, but how I do that, and what I do with it, determines what type of company I am running. I wanted the distinctiveness of that approach to be Bravery's unique selling point.

What's the biggest praise you can offer me? The dude started his company with some morals.

People tend to follow the crowd. I'd rather be a leader. That's why I chose the lion as the emblem of my company. I'd rather be a lion for a day than a sheep for the rest of my life. Male lions, especially, fascinate me. They're quite solitary creatures, since there is generally only one alpha male in a pride. They project an aura of honour, authority, dominance, power and strength, designed to deter challengers.

I've got within a couple of metres of them several times, on safari in the Kruger National Park, in north-east South Africa. They're mesmerizing. The male lion has a strut and a stride. He knows the impact of his presence. It is phenomenal to witness. There's something uniquely raw about the experience. He locks eyes with you, as if he is looking into your soul. You are hypnotized by the pin-point pupils. His stare is unwavering. He doesn't blink or flinch. He judges you, puts you in your place. He knows what he is, what purpose he serves. For all your mod cons and pretensions, you're part of his food chain.

I hear you pointing out the apparently obvious. Hang on a minute, Tobes, aren't you going over the top here? After all, you're only selling lifestyle products around extreme sports like surfing, skate-boarding and dirt biking. Bear with me, but the accessories, the branded leisure wear and the culture of the activities in which we are involved serve a broader purpose.

This isn't necessarily about product, the cool pair of sunnies or the smart skateboard deck. It's about the person. I wanted the company to be an extension of myself, part of my identity. Bravery, both the company and the concept, is about encouraging everyone to reach their full potential. Marketing people may focus on the brand, which is a shallow word and attitude, but to me its broader aim gives it authenticity, energy and relevance.

I wanted to link Bravery to youth intervention programmes, and use it as a platform to embolden individuals at key moments in their lives. That involves reminding them that by taking risks, stepping out of their comfort zones in associated activities on land and sea, they can examine their choices and attitudes.

One of my favourite passages, taken from the 'Man in the Arena' speech by former US president Theodore Roosevelt, speaks of the man 'whose face is marred by dust and sweat and blood', who 'if he fails, at least fails while daring greatly, so that his place shall never be with those cold and timid souls who neither know victory nor defeat'.

It is too easy to avoid obstacles, ignore challenges. An easy life isn't all it is cracked up to be.

The central message involves the importance of self-belief. We are on this earth to live big and not small, to confront what scares us so that we welcome fear, because we understand it. Fear is merely a feeling, a fragment of the imagination. It shouldn't be the driver of our actions. By finding bravery in small things, quiet passages, we can learn to find courage in big moments.

Sure, it can be a scary process. But it is also life-affirming. I wanted to work with extreme sports because I have always loved the outdoors, and they epitomize the benefits of ordinary people daring to be extraordinary. It takes courage to throw yourself at a huge breaking wave, or to defy gravity on a skateboard or a dirt bike, with the throttle thrust wide open, but the rewards are immense.

The experience of pushing back personal boundaries builds character, confidence and pride. When an introverted kid conquers himself by standing up on a surfboard or skateboard, the look on his face is absolutely priceless. It is as if a light has been switched on. It's so cool to see, because it is the human equivalent of a butterfly emerging from a chrysalis.

He feels visibly good about himself. His shoulders are back. He's inviting the world to check him out.

There's a basic benefit in showing someone they can achieve their goals, however ambitious they may be. They're more inclined to stand up for themselves, which in itself is a huge step forward for any kid. Children can be cruel, they can attack anyone who appears a little different, so it takes tremendous courage to be yourself.

I had to deal with that, growing up. I hate bullying with a passion because of what happened to me. It sticks with me. It is one of my bugbears. I had to be brave to step up and confront my tormentors. It was sometimes hard to get the words out in the right order because I was so nervous, but I was consistent in my defiance: 'Pick on me, mate, pull that shit on me, and see what happens. You'll learn your lessons the hard way. Walk away now.'

Sometimes they did. Sometimes they didn't. If a problem is not hard to tackle, and it doesn't test you, it tends not to be that important. I believe there is a part of us that cannot be crushed or defeated. Our spirit will endure. We all know how easy it is these days to turn a blind eye, but each of us has a capacity to help others in trouble.

Fear can be overcome with boldness and decisiveness. You must be brave enough to make the tough call when your heart tells you it is the correct course of action. Refuse to allow fear to seize control of your life. By making unflinching choices, when new challenges inevitably arise you will take small, firm steps forward.

I'm attuned to what I call everyday bravery, the type that can easily be overlooked. It tends to emerge when people feel intimidated by supposed inadequacy. I saw it quite a bit in college, where certain pupils were visibly unsettled by their struggle to grasp a particular subject. They hated their failures being magnified in class, in front of their peers, but refused to give up. They kept going. They sought and accepted help from the teachers, and tried everything within their power to improve. That's as courageous, in my book, as assisting a stranger in distress, or helping out at the scene of a car accident. You can't teach bravery, but you can develop inner strength through a value system based on the difference between right and wrong.

Perfection doesn't exist, even though in modern society it seems everyone is pushing an image of flawlessness. Those so-called influencers on social media, for instance, make me cringe. *Look at me. Look at my perfect life. Look at what you should be, what you could be.* Well, bullshit. We all have issues. Trust me, I should know.

I've been humbled by what I've seen beyond the battlefield. I'm not referring to myself here, but it takes real courage to deal with severe injuries, or to make sense of the emotional fallout of returning from the front line. It takes tremendous resolution to haul yourself back from really bad places, where pimps and pushers try to take advantage of your vulnerability.

Brave men admit they need help.

It also takes a lot of nerve to show spiritual courage, to promote your difference, whether that is philosophical, in terms of lifestyle or religion, or practical, in ignoring the critics. The easiest thing in life is just to take your place in line and hope no one notices you. What's the old saying? Stand for nothing, fall for everything.

It took me a while to work out how to make a difference, in my own small way. I found what I was looking for in a charity called Surfers Not Street Children, which was founded in 1998 by Tom Hewitt. A British activist and surfer, he has worked with homeless kids, principally in South Africa and Mozambique, but also in Burundi, Kenya, Tanzania, Sierra Leone, Ethiopia, Zambia, Nicaragua, Honduras, Costa Rica, Brazil, Peru and India. He enlisted a maverick crew of social workers, volunteers and carers, based in Durban, and used surfing as a means of social escape, into education, employment and mainstream society. The more I spoke to Tom, the greater my urge to help, in any way I could. My company's support is financial, but also logical and fiercely emotional, since his philosophy aligned perfectly with mine.

I'd seen similar children, in townships and poor rural areas, destitute and alone. They were treated as human trash – a wicked assumption, since a feeling of worthlessness destroys any semblance of hope, and encourages self-loathing. They're generally good kids, disadvantaged by a random consequence of birth and geography. So much potential goes to waste. They are beaten down, so they forget their capabilities and are unable to fulfil their promise. I loved the charity's great cause, its humanitarian purpose. I also identified with the methods involved in using surfing, a sport I know well, to break the circle of rejection and resentment.

That might seem a little far-fetched, because surfing in the UK has a privileged, middle-class image. It's almost exclusively white and not seen as a sport for the people, like football. But that's far from the case across the world, where, away from the traditional heartlands of Hawaii, Australia and the US, in places like Peru and Ghana, it is increasingly popular. The surf shack culture in South Africa is huge.

Tom's programmes in Durban, assisted by local surfing legend Sandile Mqadi and social worker Slie Ngema, who runs a girls' empowerment project, accommodate up to 120 children at any one time. A complementary curriculum in Mozambique, overseen by Mini Cho, a young surfer who once lived on the streets, looks after another fifty or so vulnerable youths. Over the years they have helped thousands find themselves.

The aim is to offer safe play, a healing space, and mentorship opportunities designed to develop youngsters into self-sustaining adults. Earning the trust of those who have no reason to trust is a long and delicate process. It can take several years before a street boy or girl finds the courage to mend their broken life and revise their seemingly hopeless future.

They are conditioned to being used and abused. Gang culture draws many into knife crime and other criminal activity. There is a massive drug dependency problem. It is pointless trying to preach at them; they need to discover for themselves the benefits of human kindness and innocent opportunity. Then, and only then, can they deal with their pain and control their destiny. That, in turn, inspires others.

True power comes from within.

What Tom calls his 'lightbulb moment' came just after the millennium, when he marshalled a successful campaign against municipal clearing programmes, in which homeless children were literally swept off the streets before major civic events such as international sports fixtures or global conferences.

One of the charity's most powerful advocates, Ntando Msibi, was a victim of the purges. Orphaned at the age of eight, he began living on the streets three years later, when he fled from an alcoholic, abusive grandmother. He struggled with substance abuse, and was a typical target for the so-called child catchers. On one occasion, ironically when Durban staged an international conference against racism, he was rounded up, beaten up, and dumped by the roadside more than 30 miles away. He had no option but to walk, shoeless and starving, back to the city, which remained his closest point of refuge. It took him more than two days. When he arrived, exhausted, he curled up in a vacant squatters' shack littered with needles discarded by drug addicts.

He gravitated towards the seafront, near the New Pier, where he begged for money and scavenged food from dustbins. By chance, he recognized a couple of slightly older street kids in the water, being taught the rudiments of surfing by a blond-haired white guy who turned out to be Tom. He saw them laughing in the waves, and had the courage to ask to join in.

Tom put him on a board, and invited him to hang out with the others in his surf club – an unofficial drop-in centre for the underprivileged. With that simple gesture of humanity, Ntando began the transformation from society's pariah, and an all-too-familiar poverty statistic, to self-confident success story.

His journey was far from simple. He was damaged psychologically, and found it difficult to kick his drug habit. Tom persevered because, in the wreckage of an impoverished boy's desperation, he recognized a true talent. Ntando now competes internationally on the surfing circuit; representing South Africa, he recently finished seventeenth in the world junior championship.

That's an amazing achievement, but just as importantly, he actively inspires others from similar backgrounds to express their talent. Andile Zulu, one of the youngsters in his orbit, is now a fully qualified lifeguard. Other former street children work in restaurants, or the retail industry. Achieving academic excellence is difficult, since most have never had formal education, but not impossible.

Tom, who was awarded the MBE by the Queen in 2011 and has the patronage of Prince Harry, has created a virtuous circle. He uses his network to provide psychological counselling, vocational skills training, and job placement services. Those he has plucked from the street have formed a think-tank which lobbies government and contributes to a global advocacy campaign.

I can't tell you how much the experience of being involved, even on the periphery, has enriched me. I know from bitter experience that wins in life are fleeting, but if I can help others find something in themselves, I will be fulfilled. In a strange way, the kids have inspired me to push back my own boundaries.

I've always had an affinity with the water, but that love is incompatible with a health and safety approach to my welfare. I'm supposed to exist in a highly monitored, carefully contained situation, governed by medical professionals. To put it mildly, that lacks the edge to which I was once accustomed. In the summer before the pandemic, I finally said sod it.

With the help of Jim Patrick and his associates, I was booked into a holiday villa in Portugal. My first port of call was the local bucket and spade shop, for two inflatables. One was the standard sunbed, the other a circular lilo. I was like a naughty schoolboy let loose at the end of term, and in no mood to listen to anyone who told me my plans were too dangerous.

Once back at the villa, I persuaded my carers to lower me, attached to my portable ventilator, on to the sunbed in the pool. My only precaution involved a bucket hat and sun cream, daubed on before I was placed alongside the sunbed, on the lilo, next to my beer. I then gave them the afternoon off, because I never have time to myself. Technically, I'm not supposed to do that, but Savannah, my partner, who is trained in critical care, was with me. The tinny was complete with straw, which Sav would flick into my mouth when I was thirsty. I had the sunnies on, and the tunes turned up loud. I lay back and caught some rays. It was bliss. That's as good as it gets for me, a moment of hope and contentment.

I was glad to be alive.

SIXTEEN

Second Chance

You've never lived until you've almost died.
For those who have had to fight for it
Life has truly a flavour
The protected shall never know.

THOSE FOUR LINES, by nineteenth-century French author Guy de Maupassant, are set in a wooden frame above my bed. His short stories highlighted the futility of war, and the pain of innocent civilians caught up in the Franco-Prussian conflict of the 1870s. He describes their powerlessness, as their lives are changed for ever by forces they cannot control or comprehend.

Fast forward 150 years, to the dog days of August 2021. I am watching the human misery of the Western evacuation from Afghanistan on TV in my lounge. Kabul airport is under siege from thousands of desperate, panic-stricken people, who push and plead with arms outstretched, even as they stumble in the open sewers which surround the compound.

So much is familiar, from the heat and grime to the unmistakable signs of trauma. Children, their faces streaked with dirt, are tearful, frightened and bewildered in the crush. Parents, wide-eyed with worry, are on the edge of hysteria. I inevitably identify with the squaddies, who, flushed and exhausted, demonstrate remarkable levels of discipline, professionalism and compassion.

It's a difficult, confusing time. They've clearly snatched sleep, either propped against a wall or sprawled on exposed concrete in a dust-covered uniform. They look haunted from trying to bring a semblance of hope and order to a chaotic scene. They're young lads, at a guess in their early twenties, thrown into a situation for which it is impossible to train.

They periodically dive into surging crowds to extract visa holders, and pass them on to transportation officials organizing evacuation flights. Babies are thrust towards them over barbed wire, in the hope they will be able to guarantee them a better life. They share their water and their rations with the refugees, just as we did with the locals on our patrols in the Sangin Valley.

The look of wonder on a kid's face when he tastes a sweet from your pack melts away suspicion. It stays with you.

This is a humanitarian mission, the consequence of deeply rooted problems these British soldiers cannot begin to solve. It's fraught with danger. As I watch them do their best to help, the military man in me feels a profound pride but a deep sense of dread, justified when a suicide bomber kills 170, including thirteen US soldiers.

News channels remind us that forty-seven thousand Afghans died in the conflict, over two decades since the world changed on 9/11, with the destruction of the Twin Towers. I was fifteen at the time, back in South Africa and settling uneasily into a new high school. It was a very hot afternoon; I couldn't wait to throw off my uniform and was sitting on the sofa, bare-chested, next to my sister

Natalie, when the TV schedules were taken over by the scenes from New York.

I couldn't believe it. I didn't think it was real. It looked like something out of a *Die Hard* movie. The weirdest part of all was that I felt so connected to it. Less than a couple of years earlier, when Mum had whisked us off to the United States, and we had a stop-over in New York before taking a connecting flight to San Diego, she'd arranged for us to go to the top of the 110-storey building.

Thinking back now, I wonder whether that was the moment destiny touched me on the shoulder. The attack on the Manhattan landmark led directly to the so-called war on terror, and indirectly to my paralysis. Military action is a thread running through my life, from my stepdad's experience in the border wars to me sitting at home, in my wheelchair, watching history repeat itself.

I'm not here to make political points, or to rush to emotional judgement about the collapse of a military campaign, but the withdrawal hit me hard on a human level. I was initially angry, like many of my mates. I felt somehow worthless. I was really moved by that eerie image of the last man on the ground in Kabul, captured in the green light of a night vision scope in body armour and helmet, walking up the rear ramp of a C-17.

I'll leave it to others to analyse the significance of the vast amount of military hardware that fell into Taliban hands. I haven't a clue whether better-qualified observers than me are correct when they foresee a poor, war-ravaged country failing to find peace. It's easier to avoid drilling down into the details of the bigger picture. Dwelling on the obvious conclusion that our intervention has changed little carries the danger of being sucked into emotional quicksand. All I know is that war, any war, is about blood and sacrifice, hurt and devastation. Rather than succumb to rage at the feeling of being used as a pawn in a giant global chess game, I'm conscious of a deep ache of sadness that it has come to this, with another cycle of repression and barbarism. Images of hunger and forecasts of famine over the winter are hard to take.

I listened to the debate in the House of Commons about the withdrawal, and was profoundly affected by a speech made by Tom Tugendhat, an MP who served in Iraq and Afghanistan. When he spoke about watching 'good men go into the earth, taking with them a part of me and a part of all of us' he touched me to the core.

You can never be completely insulated from your personal experience of combat. I lost four close friends in Afghanistan, taken well before their time. The death of such good guys was, and still is, devastating. I'm enough of a realist to know that global attention will eventually shift elsewhere, to a new crisis and a different war zone, but I still clam up at the very thought of their sacrifice.

Veterans should be very proud of what they did for the greater good, no matter how things have turned out. From 2001 to 2021, average life expectancy in Afghanistan rose by nine years; it doubled for children under five. It is not the fault of veterans that the country is riddled with corruption and remains the world's largest supplier of heroin. They did their duty for the best of reasons, and to the best of their ability.

They might have been small cogs in a huge wheel, but don't tell me they didn't matter.

If I obsess about what happened to me, it will make tonight a little longer, and tomorrow morning a lot more difficult. I will never play the victim card, and harp on about how I left my future in a foreign land. That's a self-destructive way of thinking; it won't change a thing about my life, and how I live it.

You may think I'm naive, but I like to think I made a difference in the time I was there. I tried to be a good man. I hoped I was brave. I was doing my job, and feel proud that I helped to save lives, by disrupting the Taliban's chain of command.

It was more difficult for them to organize attacks, to intimidate, and to oversee public executions. There were fewer IEDs planted, to indiscriminately kill and maim soldiers and civilians alike. Those might ultimately have been small victories, advances pegged back over time, but at least we had a go at breaking the chain of oppression.

There are still 'What if?' moments, but I'm glad that I had the initiative to leave South Africa, get the bus to Bristol from Heathrow and, eventually, take the train to Lympstone. I wouldn't change a single moment of that journey, because to do so would invalidate who I am. When I put my mind to something, I become consumed by the power of ambition. I will not rest until I complete the task.

I set off desperate to learn what the world was all about. I wanted to meet new people, experience different cultures, and see new places. I've not changed fundamentally. I've still got great dreams, and exciting visions. Who knows in what direction they will take me, and where I will end up?

Don't stop believing.

I'm not saying it will be easy, because Afghanistan does not cease to matter simply because there are no longer boots on the ground. The impact of the campaign will linger, on a wider level, for years to come. A lot of my friends have suffered from mental health problems on their return. They've seen things that cannot be erased from their consciousness.

They tend to lose sight of who they are when they leave the forces. They lose their identity, the safety blanket of brotherhood, their sense of establishment in a community. No one gives a damn what they've been through and the values they represent once they find themselves in the outside world. I'm talking about strong men here, but it's natural, to a degree, to be overwhelmed.

A lot of veterans are now leaving the armed forces later in life, when the transition is more complicated. They are proud men, who are on the edge. They need support but will never ask for help. I know this because I am one of them. If they are left alone, they will retreat into the shadows. That's a cold, unwelcoming place.

You can't just say to people, 'Crack on, do your thing and you'll be fine.' It's a much more complex process. Soldiers have a powerful sense of professional pride; they have a certain social status that disappears overnight, when they take their uniform off for the final time. It's hard to get your head around the fact you are just a faceless member of the masses.

You have to find your own way. That means redirecting the strength and belief that sustained you in the services. Realistically, it will be difficult to recreate the intimacy and intensity of the friendships you developed on tour. The certainties of the piss-up with your mates, and the petty cash chit from the clerk, are gone. You can't just go to a senior officer who will act on your behalf.

You're on your own. No one is going to babysit you. No one cares what you have done. You're at the bottom of the pile, mate.

I'm no psychiatrist, but there's an obvious dilemma in being stripped of your self-worth. *I used to be someone. I used to be part of something. What am I now? What have I become? Am I good enough?* For some of us, the shock will never ease. It's a recipe for disaster. I've seen mates struggle to cope, start to lash out. I've lost them to drink, drugs, crime.

Some have pulled themselves out of the tailspin. They've recovered, and are successful in secondary careers. You'd never know the struggle they have endured, because they've learned to camouflage emotion. Yet a piece of all of us remains with our unit. Lads are drawn towards one another, sometimes decades later, because of a camaraderie that can never be replicated.

You talk about things no one else can relate to. These guys won't judge you, because they know you better than your nearest and dearest. They accept you as you are.

That begs the biggest question: how do I see my future?

I don't want to come across as some sort of happy-clappy do-gooder, but helping others has become my primary focus. That enables me to make sense of everything I've been through. Giving something back, returning the kindnesses that have been lavished on me along the way, balances my existence. It also makes me feel good, though that's not why I do it.

I understand some of you will wonder what I've been smoking here, but we're a collective. We're all together on this fragile, beautiful planet. The only way forward is side by side. The more separated we become, the more we indulge the individual, the easier it is for society to splinter, and break down. That's a no-win situation.

Human beings are phenomenal things. Everyone has a source of hidden power, that little piece of them that makes them unique. Let's call it potential. I know the downsides, the danger of that power supply being employed negatively, but if people can tap into it in the right way and at the right time, they will thrive.

The more they fulfil their potential, the better the world will be. I'm trying (and possibly failing) to avoid being cheesy, but I think my calling in life is to help them do so. That's why one of the slogans for Bravery, my company, is 'Ignite the fire within you'. Ideas and ideals make great kindling. I'm hoping that, in a small way, I can instil the right characteristics in those around me, and serve the common good.

It's a philosophy that literally comes close to home. When I met Savannah, my partner, she wasn't in the best of places. She is so smart, so clever, but wasn't making the most of her natural assets. I kept chipping away at her, encouraging her to go to university. It was a matter of gently building her confidence, and making her believe in herself.

Once that belief took hold, she flourished. She got a great degree, and is currently studying for her Masters. She's got a fulfilling career and is happy in herself. Seeing that, every day, lifts my spirits. There is almost a sense that my job is done. I've seen something similar in other people I've counselled. It is like tending a delicate plant: give it care and attention and it will bloom.

This is difficult to articulate without coming across as a bit self-obsessed, but quite a few people I've met in recent years have told me their lives have been positively influenced by the perspective of my experiences. It's one of the main reasons I'm doing this book, which is such a direct form of communication: if one reader finds a better quality of life because of it, it has been worthwhile.

I hope my story can help someone coming to terms with paralysis.

I meet quite a few people in that situation; without exception I always recognize something of myself in them. I know how tactful I have to be in trying to form a relationship, because if I am too assertive, and they are not yet in the right frame of mind, my intervention could be counter-productive.

The last thing I want to do is come across as big-headed, but they could easily listen to me and feel intimidated. By being too rah-rah and stressing what could be achieved if only they put their mind to it, I run the unacceptable risk of them withdrawing into themselves. I've been there, remember: 'Oh my God, I'm a piece of shit. I must be worthless because I will never get close to what that guy has done.'

I'm very, very careful because I sense their fear and confusion. I know they are putting on a brave face, which will collapse the moment everyone leaves. That's when despair destroys you like a cancer, cell by cell. People usually begin by telling me, 'I'm fine, I'm good, I'm getting through it.' I've heard such throwaway lines a billion times. I use them myself.

If I feel they're strong enough, I'll confront their reality. I'll try to prepare them for the moments when their dignity has been shredded or they lie, alone in the darkness, with the weight of the world compressing their chest. I'll ask them the pivotal question: 'Do you have the strength to keep going, and the bravery to face this every day?'

It's amazing how often you see a spark. That fire has to be built and sustained. Never allow it to be extinguished, because a new lease of life is possible, however daunting it may seem. You have to stimulate the essence of the individual, that internal voice that no one else hears. We've all got one, that little Jiminy Cricket on the shoulder.

When you face a problem, or need to come to a decision, the

answer is out there. Black out the white noise which scrambles your senses and confuses your brain. Something will emerge from the interference. That might be an understanding of right and wrong, a recognition of injustice, or sudden clarity of thought. Your way forward will become clear.

That fire warms in various ways. Riza Tongston is a lovely Filipino lady, a very good care manager who met me in the Priory, at the most troubled time of my life. Our mutual understanding deepened in the three years she stayed with me, as part of my care team. She had huge ambitions to own and run her own national agency, but struggled to summon the courage to take the decisive step.

We spoke about the purity of her calling, to help others in my situation. I talked her through my thought processes in setting up my own business. Drawing so many strands together is rarely smooth. It involves a lot of persistence, a decent dollop of humility and, above all, an unblinking eye on the main goal.

Riza's dream was fulfilled. She is now an extremely successful businesswoman, as well as being a very good friend. She doesn't spare my blushes, because she openly and blatantly tells me that if it were not for the first-hand experience of seeing how I dealt with adversity she would not be where she is today. I've become a bit of a mentor to her, because she trusts my advice.

That gives me joy. By helping others to help themselves, I can lead a fulfilling life.

I know what you're thinking, and I'm embarrassed about it. I came so close to giving up on life, giving it all away. I was weak and submissive, everything I told myself I would never become. My greatest blessing is being given a second chance at life. By that I don't mean a near miss, that narrow avoidance of an accident or a calamity, but a proper chance to reset.

I didn't take that chance for five years after my paralysis. I wasn't doing myself justice. I didn't appreciate the magnitude of my good fortune until it was almost too late. I am determined to make the most of that; I'm going to smash the walls down, man. It is only when you've been there, to the very edge and back, that you appreciate how valuable and beautiful life is.

I'm very lucky still to be here and able to make a difference. To throw away that second chance, to squander the sort of opportunity that is denied to so many, would make a mockery of my existence. It would be an insult to life itself. It would sully the memory of that poor young girl whose life support machine was switched off in the neuro ITU at Queen Elizabeth Hospital in Birmingham.

She never had my privileges.

I want to use the time that I have left productively, and positively. I don't know how long that will be, and can't predict, with any certainty, the consequences of a range of medical complications, especially in the age of Covid. I guess everyone faces the prospect that tomorrow could be our last day, but for me that reality is heightened. I'm a vulnerable adult. I could fall ill, and that would be it.

Do I worry about myself? Frankly, yes. I worry about my end of days. Will I be strong enough to die honourably, with dignity and courage? This is pretty morbid, but I don't want to die scared and alone. I want, on some level, to embrace it, face up to it and say, 'Come on then, bring it on.' I can only do that if, when I'm lying there, I am proud of the man I became.

I'm under no illusions. I've seen the fear in people's eyes when they're about to die. It's the scariest, scariest thing. I'm not a religious bloke, but it is so petrifying it literally puts the fear of God into you.

To tell the truth, when I started working on this book with Mike, my collaborator, I could not have imagined sharing my most private thoughts with the wider world. I was very cagey, emotional and closed off. I was scared what people would think of me, convinced they would regard me as a bullshitter, a crackpot trying to make a buck or two out of a story.

I came from a world in which much was kept secret for a reason, so found it hard to open up. I've had to face my fears of putting myself in the public eye. Honesty has not merely been my best policy, it has been the only viable policy. I've had to become unflinching and unwavering, because I am still intensely embarrassed by my situation and the figure I cut.

People tell me not to be so silly, but it's a natural reaction. I even find going to the shops very hard. I know I'm not that big a deal. I understand that people are consumed by their own lives, and no one really gives a shit about my sensitivities. But in my mind, everyone has a speech bubble above their head: 'Look at him. Poor guy. What a shame.' That's so intimidating.

It's a crazy world, but if we all, in our small way, do something good it will be a better world. As I've said, I don't think human beings are innately horrible. We are prone to over-analysis, because of our intelligence. Since things are so mixed up, there's an obvious tendency to do silly, stupid and, occasionally, bad things. We've all been there.

In my situation, my spirit is always going to be more powerful than my body. I've made a conscious attempt to free my spirit. There's been an element of letting go, and not dwelling on things that are out of my control. Sure, bad stuff can happen, but if you don't allow it to throw you off course you can stay true to yourself.

I have never given up, on anything. That character trait has been my saving grace, because it has probably kept me alive. I still go through horrendous peaks and troughs. I've come to terms with the fact that I always will.

The trick is to recognize when you are having a good day. Enjoy that moment of clarity. Savour that little bit of happiness. Hold on to it with everything you have got. No one's life is a straight line, is it? You also need to recognize your low points. It's OK to have a bad day.

I've been lucky. I've always been very self-aware. I know my mind, understand my emotions, and can identify my trigger points. Know yourself. Know what upsets you, and what doesn't. It's OK to have a bad day.

I'm being hypocritical here, because it is not easy to live up to those ideals. I am not some all-seeing eye. Sometimes it is those closest to me who tell me to take a step back, and focus on accepting the situation as it is. There are things you can't change. I will never be as independent as I once was. Relying on people is extremely hard, especially if you are a proud, strong-minded individual. I still struggle with that every day.

I have to be fed. I have to be dressed. I literally can't do anything without asking for assistance. It has taken me a long time to get to grips with that, and I flip my lid every now and again. When I'm cursing, I try to remind myself how lucky I am to see the good in so many people. My limitations are not their fault.

I hate myself for taking my frustrations out on these generous, kind souls. That's not a state of mind you want to be in. You start looking at yourself in disgust, start questioning everything about yourself.

What kind of man am I?

It's part of being human, I suppose. You have to be kind to yourself. You have to forgive yourself. I am terrible at it. I try, but it takes years to put self-knowledge into practice. I have been forced to learn patience.

Since my injury, life has slowed to the sort of pace I have never been comfortable with. I know now I can't expect everything when and where I want it. It doesn't work like that. If you are not calm and collected, you end up being irritable and upset. Relax, and it will come. It will just take a little longer than you want.

I have had to relearn a lot of things. I am a different person now, but the essence of me remains. I still have a zest for life. I will always be a go-getter. I still challenge what is in front of me. I will always have this cheeky-chap naughtiness. In that sense, it doesn't matter whether I'm paralysed or I'm not

There are moments when I feel at peace. They don't come around often, to be honest, but when they do, they are so powerful they keep me going for a long time. I've come to appreciate the beauty in simple things that most people take for granted.

I close my eyes and I am back on a beach in Dubai, in November 2021, with Savannah, my brother Ben, his wife Camilla and their daughters, Addison and Abigail. The sun is going down. We are eating pineapple from a small table while the kids are bombing around. I can feel their life force.

Addi, who has just turned six, sings her favourite song, from the movie *The Greatest Showman*, to me. I know my life is not perfect. I know it is hard. But I am glad I am still here. I feel so emotional, because I have been reminded that life is about our tomorrows.

I look at those kids and wish I could instil in them the knowledge accumulated during my struggle. I know they are going to face adversity in their life. It is coming. I want to give them the skills and the strength to face it head on. It's a contradiction: the only way you learn is by going through hard times, but you don't want those you love to face those hard times.

I haven't suddenly reached a point where I am completely content. I still have those dark days, weeks and months where I feel I just can't do this anymore. I often question the point of getting out of bed in the morning.

One of my trigger points is predictable to the point of being clichéd. War movies, like the First World War drama *1917*, stir my subconscious to the point where I suffer really bad nightmares that stay with me for days. I identify with the characters, but the psychological damage is deeper than that.

Everything always leads back to the night I was shot. I can never get away from it. I try to dissect the trauma, make sense of it all, but my anxiety is such that it is quite common for me to have panic attacks during the night. It is horrible; the panic gets worse because I cannot move.

I take strong medication, and I am fortunate to have such an understanding partner, in Savannah. She is so kind and caring. She knows she has only to put her hand on my head and it calms me down. I try to block out all the noise. Though I cannot physically control my breathing, I imagine myself doing so,

I try to be as honest as possible about my condition. I don't always get it right, since my words and thoughts are sometimes at crossed purposes, but I believe in the benefits of talking through problems, and around coping strategies.

At my lowest point I was encouraged to read widely about the Holocaust. It became clear that survivors found purpose and meaning in their suffering. That made a profound impression on me.

If there is anything I want to pass on to others in similar situations to me, it is that you will prevail if your sense of purpose is sufficiently strong. Find fuel to keep your inner fire burning. It might feel as if your fire has been extinguished but the coals are just simmering. All you need is a bit of kindling, and a shitload of gasoline.

Things are not going to get better overnight, but over time, slowly, they will. Have faith in the process. When it is hard, and you feel life is about to defeat you, get angry, meet it head on. Otherwise it is going to beat you to your knees and overwhelm you.

Life makes it tough for a reason. If there is a new tree in the forest it has to fight for the light near the top of the canopy. Build up resistance. Excuses are easy. Reality is not. Keep fighting to your last breath. Never accept you are done. Every day is a blessing.

Keep close to those who are close to you. They don't see the injury. They are with you, regardless. That is special and powerful. Don't worry about what other people think of you, even though the doubts will recur, whatever good you do or however high the standards you set.

Take moral courage. Trust yourself. Believe in yourself. Listen to what your heart is telling you. If you follow your heart you will not go far wrong.

Debrief

IN MY DARKEST moments, when the pain intensifies, the problems multiply, and the sense of being a burden builds in a crescendo, I weaken, and allow myself to wonder whether it would have been better to die that night, in that bleak, nondescript compound in the middle of nowhere.

I know I cannot allow myself to think that way, but despair is a powerful poison that can only be neutralized by a reminder that I am not alone. I value so many people, whose stories overlap with mine, and hope you forgive the indulgence of highlighting five individuals who have done so much for me.

They are my brother, my best mate, and two men without whom I would no longer be alive, such was their influence in pulling me out of a cycle of hopelessness. The fifth individual can only be known to you as Soldier X. He knows what he means to me. This, in their own words, is the journey we have shared since I sustained my injuries.

Ben Gutteridge – The Brother

Toby will probably tell you that if you could snap your fingers, and he'd be fixed tomorrow, he'd go back out there and do it all again.

Despite the circumstances, I'd probably say, 'Yeah, go for it, mate.' In a way, I'm kind of jealous that he got to live out his passion. Not a lot of people get the chance to do what they were born to do.

The military was his boys' club, and I understand the attractions, even if the movies oversell how awesome the brotherhood is. War is not a video game, or a film with a guaranteed happy ending. It's rough out there. You might have your mate's back, but people die.

When he was in Afghanistan we experienced a strange mixture of alarm and pride. Underneath it all, we had this gnawing anxiety, wondering where he was, and what he was doing. We were waiting for a phone call, waiting for something to happen. It's not something you can get used to, however hard you try.

Toby phoned me a couple of times, after a rough day or when he was feeling homesick. We'd shoot the shit about old times, but I could sense he wasn't entirely comfortable. He never mentioned specifics, but there was something in his voice that suggested something was wrong. If I brought it up he'd just say, 'Hey, I just needed to chat.' Then he'd come back on shore leave and be right as rain.

I guess all jobs have good days and bad days, but their bad days can be really bad. When he was shot through the arm he almost walked it off as if it was nothing. He seemed to be more proud of it than worried. Seeing that sort of reaction lulls you into a false sense of security. It's disconcerting, but it makes you think, 'Well, if that is the worst thing that can happen, he'll be OK.'

I was on an early-morning flight to Cape Town from Jo'burg for a friend's wedding and didn't get the news of his second injury until I landed. My phone lit up, and it was clear that something was badly wrong. The soonest we could get a flight to the UK was Sunday, the following day. My fiancée drove the hire car to the wedding, and the rest of the day was a blur.

We didn't know what the hell was going on. We were told Toby was VSI – very seriously injured. What did that mean? Everyone was throwing around acronyms and military jargon, but that was all the information they would give us. You think the worst, because you're conditioned to watching TV and hearing about these poor buggers getting their limbs blown off.

The brain goes into overdrive. If that had happened to him, he would probably survive. So why are they saying we need to get out to see him as soon as possible? That means it must be something worse. What could that be? You overthink things, go down another rabbit hole. I decided to numb it all with alcohol at the wedding reception.

We flew straight into Birmingham. Throughout the overnight flight I was working out what body parts I had two of, so I could give one to Toby if it was needed. An eye? A kidney? A liver? All sorts of weird scenarios went through my mind. Once we arrived at the hospital, and were directed towards the neuroscience department, I raced through another set of possibilities.

Oh my God. He's got a massive brain injury . . . he's been shot in the head . . . he's been shot in the eye . . . he's had his jaw blown off.

We weren't allowed to see him before we were briefed by the doctor. He explained Toby had been shot in the neck, the bullet had destroyed his vertebrae, but they didn't know the full extent of the damage. If he recovered – and at that stage it was a massive if – he would never walk again.

They explained they had stapled his head on to strengthen it as best they could. They used bits of his hip as makeshift additions to his spine before they sewed the back of his neck together, but didn't know what else was missing. The efficiency of the blood supply to his brain was uncertain.

The prognosis was that he was unlikely to wake up. If he did so, he would almost certainly be brain-damaged. The human body is so complex, but there is a limit to what it can take. Eventually, there was no avoiding an awful conclusion: it might be better to switch his life support machine off.

Emotion takes over at a moment like that, though I tried hard to be logical. I refused to write Toby off. We had to give him every chance to fight. We had to exhaust all possibilities, step by step, before letting him go. I was in awe of the doctors' skill, but how did we know what to do until we had tried absolutely everything?

They asked me for authorization to do an angiogram, which of course I gave. It found that the right-sided arteries from the heart to the brain were blown out, but the left side was OK, which offered hope that there was sufficient blood flow. All we could do, while he was in a clinically induced coma, was wait and see.

I'm not the most religious person, and I don't think Toby is either, but as I looked at him for the next week or so, I had the feeling he was in purgatory. When he came round he told me these weird stories, of being tested by a series of challenges and having to find a magical key. If he passed, he would receive an awesome reward. If he failed, his demise, and a place in hell, was inevitable.

Even when he was brought out of his coma, I could read in his face that he wasn't my brother yet. He didn't know whether he was coming or going. We had a lot of drug-induced conversations, when he would ramble on about all sorts of crazy stuff. It was very funny, but pretty weird. His mind was blown.

The pipes, tubes and machines keeping him alive were super scary, but after a time I worked out what each of them did. I learned about feeding lines, oxygen levels and heart rates. It came as a bit of a shock when I asked what was dripping into a jar on the side of the bed. It was spinal fluid, leaking from the side of his head.

Some improvements were less scientific, and enabled us to deal with his biggest frustration: being unable to make himself understood because he could not make a sound. We look similar, and move our mouths in the same way, so I found it incredibly easy to lip-read him. The nurses could not work out that he was dying of thirst. That helped him take a small step towards taking control of his life.

The company I worked for were great. They gave me all the time I needed to work remotely from the UK for six months. It enabled me to spend the mornings and evenings with Toby. We'd had our ups and downs in the past, but it brought us together. Leaving him, to go home, was the hardest thing I've ever had to do, but it was a good thing because it was another test of his self-sufficiency.

What do they say about steel forging steel? You get harder from tough situations, and this terrible situation has brought the best out of Toby. I'm sure he would not have wanted to go through it all, but he has come out the other side. He's had some dark times. He will always have dark times. But now he knows how to work through them.

His mentality has always been to push the boundaries, and the military has given him decisiveness. He weaned himself off most of his drugs because he told himself 'I don't need this shit'. He knew the ones to keep = the ones which regulate his blood pressure, or prevent bed sores, or whatever – and took control. He could then own his life.

I don't know another human being strong enough to do that. I know I couldn't do it. He has always been a stubborn bastard, and I suppose the military has brought out his pride in getting things done, no matter what people say. Stop whining, dry your eyes and get on with it. He has a unique ability to get the best out of a situation that would overwhelm most people.

It's inherent in human nature to look twice, but I don't see his injury because he is my brother. When my three-year-old daughter plays with him, she doesn't see his wheelchair. She climbs on his lap, messes with his breathing tube, and, with that youthful naivety kids have, asks why he is always sitting down. He tells her, 'It's because I'm a little bit broken.' She says OK, and that's the end of it.

I guess that's quite special. Anyone who gets to know Toby realizes that people are more than their disabilities. He has transcended everything, and that has to be inspirational.

John Knowles – The Mate

I was at Faslane, with the Fleet Protection Group, when I heard the news. My sergeant major immediately gave me permission to go to Birmingham that weekend, to see Toby. The boys on the base saw him as one of their own. Unfortunately, that meant I arrived at the hospital after what was, for me at the time, a typically lively Friday night.

Toby tells everyone I turned up with facial cuts and two black eyes. Actually, it was only one. It probably wasn't the best look for my first meeting with his mother, Ann. I explained I'd had a bit of trouble, and she realized that all the stories she had heard, about what Tobes and I used to get up to, were probably true.

Before we went in to see him, the doctors prepared us for the worst. They said Toby might not make it. At best he would probably be in a vegetative state. All hope wasn't gone, but it was best to be realistic. The hairs stood up on the back of my neck. Something was telling me to have faith in him. I told them they didn't know the strength of the man.

It was the darkest time. Toby was alone in a room, in an induced coma. His hair was long, from specialist ops, and spread across his pillow, but it seemed like his head was hanging on by a thread. It was obvious he had suffered massive damage. There were tubes everywhere, and he had ballooned. He was in a bad, bad way.

Even now, all these years later, the memory still gets me . . .

I was desperate to control my emotions, petrified I would break down. His mum obviously sensed that and said it was OK to let go. I had a few quiet words, told him that if anyone could come through it, it was him. That was who he was, a fighter. I left him a couple of photos, one of us together and another with him in a Springboks jersey. Man, he loved his rugby.

I knew he had something special about him from the first time we met, at Lympstone. He stood out from the crowd, and was always one of the front runners in training. He had obvious qualities, like courage and determination, but also something extra, what I called Commando Strength. He was mentally tough. People wanted to be alongside him.

We got on well, since we were both rebellious, but while I did the drinking and partying, he also did the soldiering. He came up to me once, at breakfast, and started lecturing me on nutritional values. He would do anything to be better. He knew where he was going from day one, week one. His fitness was incredible, and is one of the reasons why he is around today.

I went away and had back surgery, so it was quite a few weeks before I was able to see him again. When I did, he was lying flat on his back, with a big fat smile on his face. I just burst into tears. It was amazing. The first thing he said to me was, 'I'm going to walk again.' We trotted out the old line in unison: 'If the mind can conceive it, man can achieve it.'

People use the word 'tragic' without realizing what it truly means. Toby's is a life well served. If one person who is ready to give up and commit suicide changes their mind because they read his story, he has done more than most people achieve in a lifetime. The shit he has dealt with, the strength he has shown in a terrible situation, can't help but have a positive effect on anyone who comes into contact with him.

Toby has helped me in ways he probably doesn't realize. I've had my problems with drugs and alcohol, but I've dealt with my addictions. How could I have given in to them when I see what he has done? He never looked for charity. His business, Bravery, is his brainchild. It helps others. He's not a gobby guy, but when he speaks you should listen.

He was probably among the top hundred soldiers on the planet when he suffered his injuries. It is a testament to his character that he has allowed nothing to stop his momentum. If he can be that impressive, why can't the rest of us, who have lesser problems, show the same attitude? I look at him, and take hope.

Jim Patrick – The Advocate

At the time of Toby's injury, I was chairman of the SBS Association. The operational tempo of the unit was extremely high, and we had recently suffered a number of casualties. We received notification that someone had been taken back to Birmingham who had sustained such a serious injury that he was unlikely to survive. I visited the hospital with the association's chief executive and a trustee who was a lawyer, to meet the family and transfer power of attorney.

During my career I have seen horrific injuries and I have had contact with the families of lads who have been killed, so I thought I was prepared for anything. When I was ushered into Toby's room, I saw a young, fit man lying there, naked, with just a cloth over him. The way he was lying I could not see the single bullet wound through the back of his neck that had caused such devastating damage. Apart from the breathing tube inserted, there was not a mark on him.

He was the same age as my son.

That picture will stay with me for ever.

From that instant I had a connection with Toby which has continued long after I left my role as chairman, SBSA. His prognosis improved, he refused to die, and he has kept fighting, through everything. Though he found it difficult to communicate in the early stages, he was absolutely lucid about his situation. For someone who had been so horribly hurt, that was amazing.

Over time, my experience with Toby has changed my view on

how the military operates. I spent thirty years in the Royal Navy and left as a commodore, which is a relatively senior rank. My leaving speeches contained stock lines about how great the military is in looking after its own, but I was now to find out that this is not always the case.

Looking at Toby, that night, this perfect physical specimen whose body would never work again, convinced me there had to be something we could do to make sure his life was as good as it could possibly be.

Even back then it was clear that the severity of his injury meant he would require complex care and support for the rest of his life. In the car on the way home from our first hospital visit I turned to the other guys and said we would need another funding stream for him to have anything like the quality of life he deserved.

At the time, the maximum compensation the MoD could provide was a one-off payment of £570,000. It was then over to the NHS to provide health care and support. Our NHS is wonderful and the treatment Toby received in hospital was outstanding. However, the NHS is not resourced to provide the sort of holistic health and social care that Toby would need for the rest of his life. If that had happened to your son, or my son, what would you have done? Like many parents did, you'd have dropped everything to devote your life to support him.

Toby was at the centre of a perfect storm. His family were in South Africa and therefore there was no one to take overall responsibility for his future care. We did have a conversation about him moving back, to a medical facility, but it became obvious very quickly that the system there could not meet Toby's complex care requirements. In particular, Johannesburg experienced a power cut for a significant period each day, which would have been very difficult for someone who needed a ventilator twenty-four hours a day to breathe.

When Toby was discharged from hospital in 2010 his clinical care was entrusted to a private agency commissioned by the NHS. The initial care package was woefully inadequate. Normally someone with that level of injury and ventilated would be immobile, probably spending most of the day in bed. Toby was different.

The very attributes and values Toby showed in service have made it harder for him to accept 'this is me'. He wants more. The Special Forces want someone strong, a perfectionist who will never give up. They only recruit the highest calibre, and Toby fitted the bill perfectly. I am absolutely certain that he would have been selected to apply to become an officer at the earliest opportunity.

He was the ideal specialist operator. I've seen it so often, guys with wild, youthful spirits flourishing as they mature. Toby's academic ability would have been allowed to emerge, and his career would have been outstanding. The drive that he has shown, and continues to show, tells me that.

This was a dreadful time for Toby as care package after care package broke down. No one would listen when we tried to tell them at the outset that the level of care was insufficient, and the package would not work. Over an eight-year period it has taken seven different agencies to eventually arrive at a care package fit for purpose. Things had to fail, sometimes catastrophically, before a new agency would be brought in with an improved level of provision. It was very difficult to get anyone to believe how bad things were. How could a war hero possibly be neglected in this way? Well, since leaving hospital he was desperately neglected, and in 2013 he even became the subject of a Local Authority Safeguarding investigation.

A lesser man would have given up at this point – but this was Toby. I know he had some very dark times but he always dug deep and his determination, inner strength and courage got him through.

Toby needed an overarching system of care and support around him that was holistic, would operate seamlessly, and was funded through life. He had already used the £570,000 compensation to purchase a house.

This one-off payment might have been adequate for the majority of the very seriously injured who qualified. If you've lost a limb and you get a state-of-the-art prosthetic, you can still hopefully get a job, you can move on. I know of a triple amputee who runs his own business, and one of our lads who lost his leg has gone on to be a helicopter pilot.

With Toby, it didn't scratch the surface. His situation was unprecedented. There had never been an individual with such through-life complex care requirements who would be totally reliant on the 'system', and consequently no 'system' yet existed. There was no individual or organization to take responsibility for Toby's overall care and welfare. There was no 'one-stop shop' and no single source of funding to pay for all the therapy, specialist equipment and social care requirements that fell outside the remit of the NHS. The NHS did have responsibility for Toby's clinical needs but we used to say that they were resourced to keep him alive, not give him a life.

I made the point that on the fateful night when Toby was shot no one questioned the hugely expensive state-of-the-art equipment used by specialist operators. There was no thought given to the cost of his weapons or the amount of ammunition he was issued – he was given everything he required for the task. So why was there such reluctance now to equip Toby with the appropriate level of clinical care along with the specialist equipment and support that he needed?

We, as a nation, trained this young man to protect us. We sent him to fight a war thousands of miles away, and when he returned, maimed, we abandoned him. This was wrong. We had a duty to provide Toby with the care and support he needed to gain a level of independence to give him some quality of life.

We managed to obtain funding to commission a holistic assessment of needs. This was a breakthrough and provided the evidence to articulate Toby's requirements. This enabled me to come up with the concept of an integrated care system, founded on Toby's needs, be they clinical, therapeutic or social. Money was only one part of the equation; the will to work together was decisive. We established a multi-disciplinary team in which needs are compartmentalized, and coordinated. Support from the MoD and NHS is complemented by the outreach work of a range of military charities.

To give you an idea of how it operates, when Toby gets out of bed in the morning he is transferred in a hoist, supplied by the local authority, to a wheelchair provided by the Royal British Legion. Assisted by carers funded by the NHS, he uses a shower adapted by the MoD, who also paid for the lift in which he reaches the ground floor of his house, which is partially financed by Help for Heroes, the SBS Association and an organization called Haig Housing Trust, who have looked after former servicemen for a century.

Toby doesn't need to concern himself with the separate sources of income. With good coordination and management, the various components operate seamlessly, and the impact is transformational.

It is testament to the man that Toby was determined to put something in place to make sure that no one ever had to go through the traumatic time that he did. We were delighted and very proud when the integrated care system was adopted by the MoD for injured service men and women who require through-life care.

The credit for that belongs to Toby. He has given us the power of precedent. Now when someone wakes up in hospital in Birmingham, paralysed and fearful of the future, there is a process, a system in place to offer help. That's down to him blazing that trail, refusing to give up. It's some legacy.

Toby went through hell, but I never doubted him. The resilience he showed and continues to show is an example to us all. It is great to see him today. Toby is a graduate. Toby is the chief executive of his own company. Toby isn't the wounded soldier sitting in a wheelchair – a perception I know he hated.

He is a remarkable man.

Ross Hoar – The Psychotherapist

It was a normal sort of day in the therapy office at the Priory. There was a constant flow of new cases, with differing challenges. As part of the handover I was told of a new arrival. He was paralysed and had been in the Marines. That was pretty much it, really. At face value, in the sense of Toby's physical condition, his situation didn't seem that unusual.

Toby was sitting on the far side of his room, near the nurse's station on the left-hand side of the unit. He'd just had a shower. I introduced myself, talked about what I did, and how I might be able to help. The major adjustment for me, in those first few days, involved understanding the profundity of his paralysis, and the culture from which he came.

There were awkward moments that come with the territory, like instinctively offering him a hand on getting up to leave. You have to be very conscious of language in dealing with the level of someone's disability. You try to avoid using phrases like 'putting your best foot forward' or 'stand up for yourself', but they occasionally slip out.

My impression of Toby was that he was clearly physically restricted, but also hugely locked down, mentally. He was distant, and difficult to fully assess because there were no tangible clues from his movements or mannerisms to pick up on. I'm familiar with physical disability, but I was very aware Toby was facing a phenomenal challenge, which I didn't fully understand.

Things began to click into place when I came out of Toby's room and saw a couple of people from the Marines, including what I later learned was his welfare officer, waiting to enter. It was like stepping out into another world. I'd been talking with Toby, face to face, listening to him, and trying to get to know him. Suddenly it was, 'Blimey. Who's this?'

How did they relate to the person I'd just met? How do I relate to them? The shock of two different cultures meeting like that gave me an insight into the adjustments Toby was having to make. I realized I had to connect with who he was, rather than giving him a list of things to do so that he would feel better. That would have been patronizing, and is not how I work in any case.

Toby and people like him in the military have very strong value systems. He obviously had a very strong mind that was working against itself. He was using every skill he had, every instinct he possessed, to get where he wanted to go. That strength was more frightening than any weakness. Toby didn't necessarily want to live, and if that was what he wanted that was what he would do.

In our line of work we try to normalize things. With Toby we tried to normalize the concept of limitations. Obviously, as far as he is concerned those limitations are on a completely different level, but all of us, to varying degrees, face restrictions. Introducing some element of that into our discussions helped.

Relating things to his childhood was also instructive. Culturally, growing up in South Africa, he did not have a lot of experience of people with disabilities. He didn't have the usual frame of reference of seeing someone in a wheelchair, and recognizing they were a valid human being who just happened to be physically restricted.

Strangely, probably because of the paralysis, Toby is the purest person I work with. By that, I mean pure emotionally. He cannot go anywhere, cannot get away from what he is facing. There might be times when he has had enough, but he can't hide from it. Part of the recovery process has been about opening up.

It is not about 'either or'. It's also about 'and'. Trauma is particularly black and white, so recovery is about building a degree of grey into the process. It's about being able to say, 'Yeah, I'm having a rough day and hate everybody, and there was a time yesterday when I felt all right. So I can be paralysed and have a purpose.'

Previously, Toby felt he had to physically dominate and achieve, or else he was useless. We've managed to find ground between those two polarities. I haven't a clue what it is like being in his body, and he hasn't a clue about what it is like being in mine, but we are working together at a pace at which he can process things, without pushing and forcing it.

The tipping point was having a consistent team of carers around him. My role involved having some idea of how residential care should work, not just medically but in terms of social welfare. I offered a different context, in other words not a military one, and a different voice. I wasn't there to make him do anything, or fix him. I was there to help him help himself. The relationship helped Toby trust that people were coming into his life not out of a sense of pity or charity, but with his best interests at heart. That's a significant shift. I've felt sad for what Toby has experienced, but I've never felt pity. I respect him too much to pity him.

To me, he is so, so much more than his injury. I know that is easy for me to say, but if all people see of Toby is his injury they will miss who he is.

I was recently discussing my work with him. Toby had been unwell, and I suggested that if he went into hospital, or even a hospice, it would probably be time for me to back off, and let the medical teams do their stuff. I was advised against this, since, on reflection, it was precisely the time for me to step in, be present, and ensure Toby had dignity and due respect.

Toby has lived, indeed is living, a good, fulfilled life, the best he can live. If anything was to happen to him I would feel a tremendous sense of loss. I'd lose a part of me. I have worked with people who are dying. It is a completely unique experience. I utterly believe Toby would face death with courage and dignity.

As I said, the loss, from a personal perspective, would be acute. But I would also be full of admiration for a man who was completely true to himself, who did what he did, despite everything.

Soldier X – The Brother in Arms

Toby joined the unit at the height of the Afghan campaign, straight off the back of his selection. Most guys do a couple of insertion skills courses at that point, but we were getting ready to deploy in what was a bit of a unique situation. It was a very busy tour, and our pre-deployment training was shorter than usual.

Selection is designed to get you ready to go, but it must have been quite daunting for Toby. The rest of us knew what we were going into. I've never experienced a busier time, before or since. Casualty rates were high: soldiers were losing their lives quite regularly. It's to Toby's credit that he never gave the impression of finding that forbidding.

We all effectively start from scratch in the unit, even though we take our previous military experience with us. Toby was a sponge, quietly soaking up new information. Your perspective is always listened to, but he knew the guys around him knew more than him.

Whether he was aware of it or not, he had people keeping an eye on him. We all remember what it was like as the fresh-faced young guy. The advice tends to be practical. To give a typical example, an elite soldier is allowed personal preferences in his assault gear. A newcomer usually uses the kit choices made by the more seasoned guys as a template.

Our values are forged in selection. When you are out in the field you know that the person next to you, in front of you and behind you has gone through the same process. That person has proved themselves. There is no back door into our world: I have seen some fantastic soldiers fail to make the grade. We take the cream off the top.

You can break selection down into two halves. The first part gauges physical ability. At that stage the examiners have no interest in what is going on inside your head. They are looking to see how you work in an arduous situation. Focus changes in the second half. You can be the fittest, strongest candidate, but if you lack mental robustness and tactical awareness you won't make it.

You will be overloaded with information in an extremely unpleasant environment. Everyone has doubts about whether they are going to pass the course, or whether they have the capability to push on, but they have to show strength of mind to overcome them. Determination is one of our principal attributes.

You control that metre-square box around you. The overall situation can be daunting, but you break things down into small, solvable problems. You eat the elephant one bite at a time. You progress step by step, day by day. There is an element of humility involved; you have confidence and belief in yourself without being cocky.

Guys know you can be relied on, without question. In turn, you're happy to go into battle with them because you know you can rely on them. There's the odd exception, but in general people do not fight for Queen and Country. When you are up against it, you fight for your brothers. You go the extra mile because your actions can affect the lives of others.

No one wants to go to war but it is what we train continually for.

I identified with a surgeon who said he didn't want people to be badly hurt, but at the same time he needed to perform often delicate operations to know he could still do his job.

We were flat out on that three-month tour. It felt like the longest period of my life. We weren't in big firefights every time we went out, but we were often in battle situations. That never becomes mundane, but operations seemed to merge into one another. The only reason to remember them was when something shocking happened.

During the operation that resulted in Toby's injury we were dropped off quite a way from the target, to gain maximum surprise. Moving very quietly, weaving through villages and around buildings at a steady pace, is an eerie process. Everyone's senses are working overtime.

It's entirely logical that Toby can't remember anything after we reached the target, and locked it down. I've tried to explain events to him. We were in the lead team, entering the compound. I was third through the door into the courtyard; Toby was right behind me. It was quite a cluttered scene; the living quarters were off to one side, and though our night vision goggles were very good, foliage made visibility difficult.

I went in a different direction to the first two guys, creeping along the walls to maximize what I could see. I had moved a couple of paces beyond a water butt when there was heavy gunfire, a spray from an AK-47. My instant thought was I couldn't go backwards, because Toby would need to take cover behind the butt, so I took a single step forward.

At that moment, in my peripheral vision, I could see an apparently lifeless body. Toby had fallen forward, without even putting his hands out. He had been completely switched off. It was as if someone had cut the string on a puppet. I tried to make myself into the smallest object possible, and hide in the darkness. I had no cover.

It was surreal. It was extremely difficult to identify where the gunfire had come from, but suddenly, cautiously, a door opened and a guy with an AK-47 slowly walked across the threshold. After what felt like quite a long time, but must have been only a couple of seconds, he heard a noise and raised his rifle.

There was no choice but to eliminate him. Here was a man who had fired at us, hitting Toby, and would 100 per cent have done so again. He fell backwards into the room; the door swung shut. Tactically that made the next couple of minutes difficult: it would have been easier if he had fallen forward.

It at least meant we were able to drag Toby outside the compound, where a medic and some of the team patched him up as best they could. He was not breathing but he did have a pulse. A few of us advanced to clear the building, to make sure no one else was around. As we did so, explosives detonated and forced us temporarily off target.

Evidently, the individual who had been neutralized was a very bad guy.

Our mission swung to extracting Toby. The Chinook carrying a doctor was called in, and a landing site secured. I was on one corner of the stretcher at the head end. People talk about a dead weight; it was incredible how heavy he felt as we carried him, on the run, across a ploughed field. He was still being bagged, to force air into his lungs.

Our boots were caked in mud and our muscles burned. As we

tried to get him up the tail ramp we almost dropped him, but he was dragged on board. Effectively, we were delivering a body to be taken home. I stayed on the ground, thinking we would not see Toby again. To be honest, none of us expected him to survive.

It's a deeply personal process, but formalities had to be observed at our base, where we gathered Toby's belongings, placed them into a bag, and packed his room up. It was between twelve and twenty-four hours after we returned that we learned he had not died, but was in an induced coma.

The next update came a day later. The worst-case scenario was that Toby would be 100 per cent paralysed, unable ever to speak again. There was a good chance he would be trapped in his own head. Even if his brain was functioning he might only be able to communicate by blinking.

That had a huge effect on us. It still makes me emotional to think about it. Our actions had helped keep him alive, but should we have left him there instead of letting him live a life you and I, and more importantly he, might not want? As selfish as it seems, those thoughts do go through your head.

Of course, I'm pleased we did save him. He's a fantastic man. Bravery isn't necessarily a physical act; the courage and strength Toby has shown since his injury is a state of mind.

If I'm honest, when I first went to see him in hospital in Birmingham, with one of the other guys who saved him who I'll call Soldier P, it was absolutely horrendous. He was in a tiny room, with only a small window behind his head, on a ward with other extremely seriously injured civilians around him. It was not a good place to be. We spent a couple of hours with him. It was winter time, and to be honest, I couldn't wait to get out and breathe the cold air. The best thing he ever did was get out of there, however long it took.

I often visited him in hospital in Salisbury. On one occasion I saw a flash of the old Toby, sitting in the sun in a quadrangle and burning to a crisp. He loved it. But when he returned to live just outside the camp, with the best of intentions from everyone around him, it must have been incredibly difficult. His back garden looked on to the camp; he heard the helicopters taking off and landing.

His community was still operating, without him. That tour had affected a lot of people. We had no option but to carry on, as we knew we would soon be deployed again. The operational tempo was incredibly tough. It sounds horrible, but someone like Toby, who had taken a headshot, was a reminder of what could happen to you. It stimulated deeply suppressed feelings.

Toby has had his problems, but I've got a lot of friends who have struggled when they've left the unit, either through injury, medical issues, or service time. The transition is scary. The unit means everything to you. It is the world's most exclusive team, but the day will come when you are someone who used to be someone.

I know when my exit date is. I am getting myself mentally prepared for the reality of it all. A young thruster will come in behind me, and I will be replaced. The Service will carry on. There will be someone else around to do something pretty spectacular. As my wife told me the other day, I just peaked too early in life.

I only need to look at Toby if I need an example of what is possible, once the uniform is packed away. That's why, over the years, I have encouraged him to write this book. The message of his story, the meaning of his determination, is profound. Face your fears. Deal with them head-on. There is a light at the end of the tunnel, however faint it may appear. There can be positives, even in adversity.

I'm proud to call him a friend. His courage is an inspiration to me and, hopefully, to many others.

ACKNOWLEDGEMENTS

One of the ironies of giving an insight into an understandably secretive world is that I am unable to fulfil completely the purpose of this section of the book, which is to name names, and thank the individuals and institutions which have made me who I am.

That said, I must begin by underlining my enduring debt to the Special Boat Service, and my respect for its personnel, past and present. Without the professionalism, courage and resilience of members of my Squadron I would not be here today. I thank them for continuing to welcome me into the brotherhood.

That's why it means so much to me that this is only the second book to be officially supported by the Special Boat Service Association (the first was the official history of the regiment.) The assistance offered to veterans by the Association's staff and patrons is beyond the call of duty. Will S, the current CEO, and welfare officer Andy W are my rocks.

Military life has shaped me, and I've tried to live the values instilled by the Royal Marines, whose welfare officer Gordon Hickin was so helpful. I've been inspired by the leadership of Gordon Messenger and Mark Lancaster. Helen Helliwell, at the Ministry of Defence, and Simon Adamson and David Palmer, retired members of the Clinical Commissioning Group, were important allies.

I owe everything to the diligence, wisdom and kindness of Jim Patrick, CBE. My everyday life has also been immeasurably improved by Carol Betteridge, OBE, the head of Clinical and Medical services for the Help for Heroes charity. I hope I've done justice to the work of Canine Partners, who supplied my four-legged soulmate, Wogan.

Similarly, I've tried to put into words how indebted I am to Gill Akhurst, my personal assistant. My current care team are exceptional. I'm grateful for the friendship and professional expertise of Ross Hoar, Nigel Smith, John Willingale, Riza Tongson and Rob Rosselli. Pete Bennett was there for me in my darkest hour. My brother, Ben, literally saved my life. I'd like to thank the rest of my family, and a wider circle of friends, for all they've done for me over the years.

This book is a team effort. Mike Calvin and I have worked on it for nearly eighteen months. In that time our relationship has deepened, so that professional and personal boundaries have become blurred. He told me at the outset that we would visit some dark places, but the experience has been enlightening and fulfilling.

We would like to thank Henry Vines and his team at Transworld, which includes Steph Duncan, Dan Balado, Tom Hill and Lilly Cox. We are also grateful for the guidance of Rory Scarfe and Jordan Lees, our literary agents at The Blair Partnership. Christine Preston, who transcribed countless hours of often emotional interviews, was with us in spirit all the way.

Mike has been through this process many times before, but it still requires the tolerance of his wife Lynn and his children, Nicholas, Aaron, William and Lydia, who have to put up with his distracted behaviour when he is in writing mode. Since I dote on my nieces,

Addison and Abigail, I relate to his devotion to his grandchildren, Marielli, Michael, Jesse and India.

On that note, I want to end by thanking my partner Savannah for her love and understanding. I can be difficult to live with, and I'm soothed by her reassuring presence and caring nature. I'm so lucky that she is at the centre of my universe.

ABOUT THE AUTHORS

Toby Gutteridge left a difficult and destructive childhood to join the Royal Marines, before becoming one of the youngest-ever recruits to join the Special Boat Service. In November 2009, he was shot through the neck during an operation in Afghanistan, and his life changed for ever.

Today, Toby runs Bravery, an extreme sports brand that aims to support and empower those who have dug deep within themselves to overcome their own adversities by finding courage, strength and the resilience to bounce back stronger than ever.

Michael Calvin is an award-winning writer and *Sunday Times* best-selling author, whose books have been hailed for their insight and influence. He has collaborated with such celebrated sportsmen as Sir Alastair Cook, Dylan Hartley and Gareth Thomas.